"Thanks for the honest a̶ ̶ ̶ ̶ ̶ *ng Out* is exactly what I need to help me figure out some important things!"

> Ashley J., age 16
> Wichita, KS

"I love the Think It Through sections! It's a fun way to look at some really tough teen questions."

> Kelsey L., age 15
> Bayport, NY

"All the short stories could be kids I know! For doctors, these two really seem to know what's going on in the real world with teens. *Hang-Ups, Hook-Ups, and Holding Out* gets it!"

> Nicole J., age 15
> Charlotte, NC

"I'm finally getting real answers to questions I've been too embarrassed to ask. It might scare some adults, but this is real life stuff for teens."

> Madison M., age 15
> Simpsonville, SC

"What a tremendous resource for girls and anyone who cares about them. Doctors Holmes and Hutchison convey solid information about girls' sexuality and other crucial topics in a way that kids will relate to. I hope every girl—and every parent of a girl—reads this."

> David Walsh, Ph.D., author of
> *Why Do They Act That Way? A Survival Guide
> to the Adolescent Brain for You and Your Teen*

girlology®

Hang-Ups, Hook-Ups, and Holding Out

Stuff you need to know about your body, sex, and dating

Melisa Holmes, M.D. and Trish Hutchison, M.D.

Health Communications, Inc.
Deerfield Beach, Florida

www.hcibooks.com

Library of Congress Cataloging-in-Publication Data

Holmes, Melisa.
Hang-ups, hook-ups, and holding out : stuff you need to know about your body, sex, and
    dating / Melisa Holmes and Trish Hutchison.
        p. cm.
    Includes bibliographical references.
    ISBN-13: 978-0-7573-0586-3 (trade paper)
    ISBN-10: 0-7573-0586-5 (trade paper)
    1. Teenage girls–Sexual behavior–United States.   2. Teenage girls–United States–
Attitudes.   3. Sex instruction for teenagers–United States.   4. Hygiene, Sexual–United
    States. I. Hutchison, Patricia. II. Title.
HQ27.5.H65 2008
613.9071'273–dc22

                                                                                    2007016611

HCI, its logos and marks are trademarks of Health Communications, Inc.

Publisher: Health Communications, Inc.
        3201 S.W. 15th Street
        Deerfield Beach, FL 33442-8190

Cover and Inside design by Larissa Hise Henoch
Cover illustration by Emily Eldridge
Interior design and formatting by Lawna Patterson Oldfield

Contents

Introduction

Authors' Note to Parents

We hope you'll read this message before you thumb through the book and get scared off by its contents. This is a book of questions and answers with some real-life stories mixed in. We want you to know that the questions in this book were asked by suburban high school girls. Some were asked at church programs, some at school programs, and some in the privacy of a medical appointment. Most of the questions we present in this book were asked on multiple occasions, indicating that these questions are almost universal in teen girls' minds.

As physicians and as mothers ourselves, we want to share with you why we think frank and complete answers are appropriate and necessary for your daughters. First, there is a lot of misleading and just plain wrong information out there. Much of it is on the Internet and television, where teens spend inordinate amounts of time. A lot comes from their peers—again, misleading and sometimes dangerous.

As the founders of Girlology, a program that primarily aims to improve family communication about healthy sexuality, we believe that knowledge is power, even when it comes to sex and other topics we'd like to shield from our children. We've learned that teaching children and teens about sex and sexual issues allows them time to process the information *before* they are personally faced with a difficult decision; without knowledge and forethought, they can be easily caught off guard. A teen who has learned about sexual behaviors and real-life scenarios has time to think about how a similar situation might personally affect her. Given information and time to process it, she can decide proactively how she would handle a sexual proposition or similarly risky situation. Then, if (or more likely *when*) she is faced with one, she is more likely to make a decision based on her values and her personal goals, rather than spontaneously saying "Sure, whatever!" because it sounds fun and exciting at the moment.

All of our teens are flooded with sexual messages every day. To think that we can shield them from it is naive. Our best strategy is to use the sexual messages we see and hear to start conversations and help our girls decide how they want to handle themselves sexually as they gain greater and greater independence. Making demands and saying "You will act this way" is fine for young children, but teens will soon be "out there" on their own. They need to know how to think, decide, and act on what is important to them. They need guidance in establishing their personal values, **but in the end, the choices are theirs to make.** If they are given the opportunity to thoughtfully and individually establish their personal goals and claim them as their own, they can be much more successful in sticking by them.

Let your daughters arm themselves with knowledge. Then engage them in mature conversations and help them make personal decisions after considering options and consequences. That sort of guidance will help you raise a thinking daughter who will apply these skills in many areas of her life. We hope this book helps.

Authors' Note to Teens

If you're a teen and you bought this book yourself, congratulations on looking for information that can help you stay healthy as you face a world full of confusing and often wrong information about your health and sexuality.

If a parent or adult who cares about you bought you this book, your first reaction might be to roll your eyes, toss it aside, and say, "I know all this stuff already." But wait! You need to give that adult some credit, because this is a tough book for parents to give to their daughters. It has information on stuff many parents don't even want you to think about, much less understand in detail—like good sex, casual sex, and date rape. It's also full of details about things like birth control, sex-related infections, and even Internet porn. Do you think the adults in your life want to have conversations with you about this stuff? No?

Believe it or not, they probably do. A lot of them just don't know how to get your attention, start the conversations, or make it real for you. So we're trying to help.

In *Hang-ups, Hook-ups, and Holding Out,* our goal is to give you honest, fact-based information about your body, guys, sex, and relationships. It's important for your health, both physical and emotional. How do we know what matters? We're doctors who have taken care of thousands and thousands of teen girls and young adult women. We know what's out there, and we've seen the best and worst of how sex affects the lives of teenagers and adults.

In this book, we've taken real questions that have come from real teenagers we've treated and talked with in our Girlology programs. As you read through the book, we hope you'll share it with an adult in your life who you can talk to about these things, or, if not a parent, maybe another relative, a friend's parent, a teacher, counselor, youth leader, or a coach.

It's important to be able to talk with a trusted adult, because your friends, as great as they are, are in the same situation as you. They're also trying to figure out all this sex stuff. Some adults haven't figured it all out yet either, but at least they've been through a lot and understand more than you think.

As a teenager, you are a sexual being. It's easy for us to say, but really, really hard for your parents to acknowledge. Does that mean we think you are having sex? Not necessarily, although we know some are. But we do know that you are curious about sex, have sexual urges sometimes, have probably looked on the Internet for some information about sex, and have probably talked with your friends a lot about what's sexy and what's not. How do we know that? It's pretty universal for teens to be curious about it. Your whole body has been developing sexually, so it's no wonder you think about it.

We believe that **curiosity is normal and knowledge is power.** We want you to know the details, the nitty-gritty, the long and short, the nuts and bolts, the lowdown and the up-and-up about sex and all the stuff that goes along with it. Why? Because we want you to have accurate information that can help you decide what is right for you. Besides, you're going to get the information somewhere, and we'd prefer for you

to get accurate information and advice that is based on medical facts—
not myths.

Each chapter in the book includes a section called "She Did What?!,"
which has real-life stories that you can probably relate to. The names of
the girls and guys in the stories are made up, but the stories are real.
Along with the stories, we've included the most frequently asked questions we've heard from real girls day after day in our offices and on our
website. We've also included sections called "Think It Through" that
help you do exactly that: think about the different options and possible
consequences for each of these real-life dilemmas. If you face all your
own big decisions and dilemmas with a personal "Think It Through,"
you'll end up making better decisions in many areas of your life. So anyway, you can read the book cover to cover, or use the chapter topics or
index to find specific information. Just read on!

Chapter

"Will I Ever Have a Boyfriend?"

Guys: the good,
the bad, the drama

A Real-Life Dilemma

"**S**ydney, that is so cool! I mean, no way, my best friend has not only been on two dates with Aidan Scofield, like the hottest guy in school, but I heard he asked you out again! I would so kill to be you," Chelsea gushed, swiping another fry through Sydney's ketchup.

Glancing up, Sydney offered a tentative smile, swirling a plastic spoon through a glob of chocolate pudding. "Yeah, we're going to the lake on Friday," she said with a shrug.

"Well, you're never going to look like her if you don't lay off the carbs," advised Amanda, grabbing Chelsea's lunch tray and sliding it to her side of the table.

Sydney glanced around the busy cafeteria. The steady hum of the entire junior class infected the air. And it seemed they were all saying one thing: *I know exactly why Aidan Scofield asked you out again!*

"Leave her alone," Sydney snapped, shoving the tray back to Chelsea. "Being me isn't all it's cracked up to be."

"What are you talking about? Even I might ditch an SAT prep class for Aidan Scofield," admitted Amanda, who was singularly devoted to her grade-point average and other points of perfectionism.

Oh, I doubt that. You'd never compromise your principles like I did . . . not even for Aidan Scofield, Sydney thought to herself.

"Didn't you have a good time at the concert?" Amanda asked. "I've never heard of any guy springing for such awesome tickets on a second date!"

"Yeah, Aidan *and* a rock concert. Zach wouldn't go for anything like that in a zillion years, and we've been dating for months. I bet he's the perfect boyfriend," Chelsea sighed, gnawing on a tattered fingernail. "So tell us, is Aidan as hot up close as he is in the hallway? Half a school year of nothing and then boom! How did you finally get his attention, Syd?"

A tray dropped onto the cafeteria table with the weight of a world history textbook, pizza, and a salad with dressing morphing into an unappetizing mess. "She knows exactly what got his attention. The sure way on to Aidan Scofield's top-ten list," accused Tasha Hart, the last member of the tight-knit foursome. "Tell them," she said, plopping down in a chair. "See if they agree with what I told you."

"Shut up, Tasha! I told you that in confidence."

"And I told you that you were crazy to let it happen again. Now I hear there's a third date? Maybe if you won't listen to me you'll listen to them. See if Amanda and Chelsea think Aidan Scofield really cares about you . . . or just the service you're willing to provide."

• • •

Two Weeks Earlier

"I thought we were going to see *Beautiful Disaster,*" said Sydney, looking around the barren theater. It didn't really matter, for all she cared, they could sit through a documentary on global warming. She was on a date with Aidan Scofield. *Her,* Sydney Landon, Lakeside High junior class treasurer, National Honor Society nominee, and now the envy of every girl in school.

"Ah, yeah, I tried to get tickets online, ahead. They were sold out. I hope you don't mind," he said, grasping her hand as she edged toward the middle of the theater. "Here, let's sit here."

He led her down a back row, his hand wrapped snuggly around hers. Sydney floated into the seat, picturing Aidan holding her hand, walking through the hall at school. Could it get any better than that?

Apparently it could. Ten minutes into some totally lame movie, with subtitles no less, Aidan's arm was around her shoulder, his mouth hotly on her neck, her lips. God, he even kissed as good as he looked. And he smelled just like the guy in the Desire aftershave ads—she was sure of it. As his hand roamed from her waist to her breasts, Sydney was especially glad she bought that satiny push-up bra. Compared to the other girls, it made her feel like she had a little more to offer in that department. Not that he'd get a chance to see any of it. She didn't do stuff like that, certainly not on a first date.

But Sydney began to wonder what Aidan might expect when his hand dropped from her breast, smoothly shifting hers into his lap. "You know, there's, um, lots of stuff you can get away with in a dark theater," he murmured in between kisses that were making her head a little dizzy.

"Yeah, like what?" she asked, intrigued by the game and impressed with herself, how much she turned him on—judging by the bulge in his jeans anyway.

"Did you know that you have the most incredible mouth, Syd, like a model or something. I, um, I've been thinking about it . . . a lot lately."

"Yeah, and what have you been thinking?" Clearly, she was a better kisser than she'd given herself credit for. Aidan's fingers tangled tighter through her hair, pulling her closer.

"I was thinking," he whispered as his hand slipped under hers, unbuckling his belt and quickly unzipping his jeans. "I was hoping you'd use it to, um, you know . . . " The kissing stopped, Sydney backing away a few inches, maybe to clear the spell he had her under. "I mean, if you don't want to, it's okay," he said as fast. She smiled, a wave of relief rolling through her. "We can just go home instead."

"Oh . . . no, I . . . well, it's just that I've never, um, I've never really done anything like . . ." Her words trailed off. What a stupid thing to admit.

"Really?" he said, that to-die-for smile lighting up, even in the darkened theater. "It's no big deal. It's not that different from kissing. . . . And you're a really good kisser, Syd. I'd consider it an honor to be the first guy you go down on."

Sydney's face grew hot, suddenly feeling cornered in that giant, empty theater. He was Aidan Scofield, the most amazing thing that had ever happened to her. And if she didn't do it, no doubt, it would be the last—the last of him anyway.

Doc Talk:
The Way **We See It**

EVER HEARD A STORY LIKE THIS ONE? Been a character in a story like this? Situations like this seem to come up pretty often in high school, and sometimes even beyond that. Why do some girls get so infatuated with a guy that they'll do *anything* (including things they never intended or even wanted to do) to make him want to hang with them? Do you think Sydney knows Aidan very well? Is this the start of a good relationship? Is it a relationship at all? Can she improve her situation, or is it hopeless already?

Relationships are tough to understand and can be even tougher to be in. To onlookers, a couple may appear perfect for each other, but what happens in the couple's private times will really determine the quality of a relationship. If the emphasis in the relationship is all physical, like with Aidan and Sydney, there's usually no emotional connection or growth. Isn't that what a relationship is *really* supposed to be about? Getting to know each other and like each other for who you *are* and not what you *do*. **The ultimate goal of a real relationship where romance is growing is to trust, respect, and care about each other in a like-never-before way.**

When you place too much emphasis on "what" you are dating (hottie, jock, rocker, popular guy) or how it looks to other people, you'll find yourself developing bad relationship habits that can stick with you for a long time. You'll do things that aren't really YOU, and sometimes you'll even forget who you really are and what you really stand for. That makes you do things you regret. It's easy to fall into a bad relationship and find yourself struggling to change it or get out of it. And it can be a really helpless feeling.

Being in a good relationship can be hard, too. **Building a good relationship actually takes a lot more work than just letting a bad one happen.** Strong relationships require more confidence, more commitment to your values, and more honesty and communication. Even in the best relationships, difficult situations and decisions will come up, so having a good foundation is important.

The first step to building a good relationship is to respect and love *yourself*. Sounds a little cheesy . . . okay, a lot cheesy, but it's true. If you don't like yourself or respect who you are, you can never expect someone else to like or respect you.

Building an honest relationship from the beginning will make it stronger and more mature. It doesn't mean there will never be problems (there will always be challenges in relationships), but it means you'll be more prepared to handle the ones that come up. So take the time to figure out what's important to YOU in your relationships, and stand up for what you believe in and want for yourself.

And one last thing: teen guys see romance and relationships a lot differently than most teen girls do. Girls see it as all too real, and guys sometimes don't see it at all. So how do you learn? Enjoy your friendships with guys and get to know how they think. Sometimes they're just into the physical stuff. Sometimes they are just trying to learn how to relate to a girl. Sometimes they're just not as interested in "a relationship" as you are. It helps to learn a guy's perspective so you can keep your own perspective more realistic.

The questions in this chapter show just how great, yet confusing and challenging, relationships can be. Read on. You may find some situations that seem familiar, or you might read something that helps you build a stronger relationship in the future. If you still have questions that we haven't answered here, check out our website at www.girlology.com. You can find more answers to other questions or e-mail your own questions to us. We'll put some of your questions and our answers on the site.

"I said the L word and my BF said nothing. Now what?"

Quickie Answer: Now . . . you're probably embarrassed, mortified, or feeling hurt. But don't be.

The Full Scoop: First of all, teen guys don't like to talk about their emotions. In fact, the part of their brain where they feel emotions isn't even connected very well to the part of their brain that handles language . . . so they don't even have the "wiring" to allow such a discussion. **This doesn't mean guys don't feel emotions, so don't give up.** Your BF may love you, but doesn't express it in words. He might instead express it in the way he respects you, looks at you, or does things for you.

He might not have responded to you because you said it early in the relationship and he isn't even sure whether he likes you, much less loves you. It sometimes takes guys longer to get a handle or put a label on their feelings.

The other thing to consider is why you are using the L word. Is it to justify why you are sexually involved with him? Is it to make him feel more committed to you? Is it to get a response out of him? Is it to establish an exclusive relationship? Remember that true love takes time to grow. Give him time to think about it, and don't expect your emotions to happen at the same exact times. Allow time and opportunities for your emotional intimacy to grow, and the feelings will become more obvious.

Finally, if you're in love and he's just not, you may need to reevaluate your relationship. Too many girls will do anything to keep a BF. Recognize that some relationships just aren't going to happen, and you can't force them. You can't make someone have feelings that they just don't have, no matter what you do.

"Why do some guys get so jealous?"

Jealousy is a funny thing. Not ha-ha funny at all, just confusing. As guys enter their teens and have all that testosterone (that's the male hormone that is responsible for things like sexual feelings, aggression, and feeling "manly") flowing in their veins, the testosterone makes them become a bit territorial—"Stay outta my space; keep your hands off my stuff!" **That's all fine if they want to be like that, as long as they're talking about stuff and not people.** People are not property that you own or control. The bottom line: anyone who acts territorial about someone else needs to get a clue. A guy has no right to be territorial about his girlfriend. She is not his "property."

So what is jealousy? Jealousy happens when someone gets territorial and feels like the "owner" of a person.

For young teen guys, a first girlfriend may actually feel like a "prize" or something he "owns." You need to help your guys realize that you can be considered a prize but that you are nobody's property. You should be able to speak to anyone, spend time with anyone, and have some time to yourself without him getting jealous.

On the other hand, girls and guys both need to respect their relationship by being faithful and honest. If you are in a relationship with one special person, there are certain behaviors that are expected. Just because you're nobody's property doesn't mean you can flirt with, make out with, or disappear with someone else and expect your BF to be okay with that. If he gets upset over something like that, he has a right to be angry and hurt. That's not necessarily being jealous. But if you're just talking to a guy friend and your BF has a fit and tells you to never speak to him or any other guys again, then you're dealing with bad jealousy and a person who wants to control you, not get to know you. **Don't allow yourself to be treated like anyone's property.** Jealousy is NOT romantic—it's dangerous. Guys who never learn how to get over jealousy can become physically and emotionally controlling and even abusive (see Red Flags on page 13). Remember that true love is not jealous.

"At what age can I have a serious relationship?"

The Full Scoop: First, let's talk about serious relationships. To us, a serious relationship is one that involves commitment, trust, honesty, respect, and intimacy. That's a lot. Most of these are easy to understand, but let's break it down. Commitment means you are willing to remain dedicated and loyal to your partner for a long time, even when the relationship is difficult. Trust means you have faith and confidence in each other's commitment and feelings. Honesty is easy. You are both truthful. The cool thing about honesty is that **when there is trust and commitment, you can be honest about things like your values and beliefs without worrying that he'll lose interest in you.** Next comes respect. When you respect someone, you value him for who he is as an individual. He may not be exactly like you, but you respect the qualities that make him unique. That also means that he respects you for who you are and what you believe. Finally, intimacy is a big part of a serious relationship, but there are two types of intimacy involved.

Physical intimacy is easy to define. It means you are physically touching each other in intimate or personal ways, and it usually refers to touch that creates sexual desire. **Emotional intimacy is more important in a relationship,** but also more difficult to describe. Emotional intimacy is being able to share your innermost thoughts, secrets, and dreams without feeling shame, fear, or embarrassment. That takes a pretty close and trusting relationship. That also takes time to develop. You don't just become emotionally intimate in a week because you decide you like someone. Emotional intimacy develops over time after lots of talking and sharing. Becoming emotionally intimate also means you are honest, trusting, trustworthy, committed, and respectful. See how it all works together?

Now that you know about physical and emotional intimacy, we want to tell you that it's **really important to have emotional intimacy before you get physically intimate.** That's not how a lot of teen relationships happen, though. The reason we think it's so important to develop emotional intimacy first is that it's the only way to know you are in a relationship where you can communicate your sexual boundaries and trust that your partner will respect them without changing his feelings toward you. Remember that **sex is supposed to be something that enhances a good relationship, not something that creates a relationship.**

So what was that question, again? Oh yeah, how old do you need to be to handle a serious relationship? Sixteen? Eighteen? Twenty-one? We don't have an age answer, but you need to be old enough to understand and handle all the things we mentioned above. And you should probably be at least as old as your parents think you need to be before you can date.

"Is there such a thing as a normal relationship?"

You probably will never see two relationships that are exactly alike, but there are a lot of qualities that make a relationship "normal." Instead of the term "normal," though, we prefer to use the terms "healthy" and "unhealthy." Healthy relationships are those that allow each individual to feel respected, valued, and free to honestly express themselves. **In a healthy relationship, neither person feels the need to change their personality, beliefs, or values to make the other person happy.** They like and respect each other for exactly who they are. There is a level of comfort that allows each of them to share private thoughts and dreams without worrying about being teased or rejected.

In unhealthy relationships, one of the partners feels more powerful or in control of the other person. There is usually dishonesty, jealousy, or a lack of respect. These types of relationships are not only unhealthy from an emotional perspective, they can also be just plain dangerous. As we mentioned in our first book, *Girlology: A Girl's Guide to Stuff That Matters,* you should be on the lookout for "red flags" in your dating relationships. Just like a red card in soccer means out of the game, red flags in dating relationships mean out of the dating game . . . now! Here's a review of the red flags to watch out for:

✳ Is he overly jealous? (Remember, love is not jealous, so don't fool yourself into thinking he just likes you soooooo much if he gets jealous too easily.)

* Does he get angry or jealous if you even talk to another guy?
* Does he frequently make you feel guilty if you do things with your friends or your family instead of him?
* Does he use crude or disrespectful language when talking about girls or women in general?
* Is he mean to animals?
* Does he like to start fights or act like he will?
* Does he blame you when he gets angry?
* Is he EVER physically rough?
* Does he use insulting words toward you or your friends?
* Does he embarrass you in public?
* Does he push you to do things sexually that you are not ready for?
* Does he cheat, steal, or use drugs?

All relationships have good times and bad times, easier times and harder times. The way you and your BF deal with the more difficult times says a lot about whether you are in a healthy or unhealthy relationship. **If you find yourself in an unhealthy relationship, you have to find the courage to get out,** even if it means losing a BF and being "alone." It might even make you feel like a loser, but in reality, the disrespectful partner is really the loser, and you will be the winner for standing up for what's best for you. For more advice on getting out, see page 27.

"How can I show my BF how much I love him without having sex?"

The possibilities are endless . . . how much time do you have?

So glad you're thinking that way! There are soooo many ways you can show your BF you love him or care a lot about him, without having sex. Certainly, you can tell him, but **sometimes guys get a little freaked out by the L word.** Showing him might just be better. Try some of the following ideas, and then see what you can come up with yourself.

* Do something together that neither of you have done before . . . go hiking, rock climbing, fishing, sailing, skating, skiing, snow-shoeing, kayaking . . .

* Watch his favorite movie without rolling your eyes.

* Learn how to give a great scalp and neck massage.

* Check out a book on his favorite sport and brush up on the rules.

* Give him a foot rub and pedicure (that takes real love!).

* Write a poem or song—it doesn't have to be about love; make it funny and catchy.

* Download his favorite music mix for his iPod.

* Paint a picture of something special to you both.

* Frame a photo or make a scrapbook of a place the two of you have been.

✳ Play board games.

✳ Take dancing lessons.

✳ Read a book out loud together and take turns reading.

✳ Volunteer together to help others. For ideas, check out Habitat for Humanity, local shelters, animal shelters, children's centers, retirement homes, community beautification projects, or just search for "volunteer opportunities" in your hometown or on the Internet.

✳ Build a model airplane and go fly it.

✳ Take self-defense classes.

✳ Perfect your kissing skills without going any further.

✳ Keep a journal together. List all the great things you do together and keep a list of things you want to do.

✳ Dance.

✳ Make him something—anything. How about cookies, a blanket, a special pillow, monogrammed socks, or a piece of jewelry.

✳ Take a photography class together.

✳ Get to know his family.

✳ Find out what he loves to do more than anything and do it with him (unless it's sex, of course!).

Now that we've started the list, you can keep adding to it.

"How will I know when I'm ready to have sex?"

The Full Scoop: This is one of the most important questions you can ask yourself. Even if you've already had sex before, it doesn't mean you have to keep having sex with every guy you date. You should still make decisions about the next time. And if you are comfortable talking with your parents or other trusted adults in your life, it's important to get their opinions as well.

For way too many girls, sex just happens without considering whether they are ready for it or not. And the majority of teen girls who have sex say they wish they had waited. Why? Once you start having sex, you open a whole new world of worries and vulnerabilities. So how do you know when you're really ready and you won't have any regrets?

You have to start planning *now*.

That means you need to start deciding what is important to you when it comes to sex and relationships. It makes perfect sense to want to be in a long-term, committed relationship where you and your partner know each other better than you know anyone else, trust each other, and love each other. For girls, those feelings may come earlier than they do for guys. In fact, for guys, it's hard for them to really care about a girl in that kind of way until they are in their late teens to early twenties.

We're not just randomly using those ages to scare you into waiting. Scientific research actually tells us that in general, **boys' brains take longer than girls' to develop the parts that make them understand emotional intimacy, romantic feelings, and commitment.** They just aren't very capable in the "committed relationship" area until they're older, because that part of their brain hasn't finished developing until then. For that reason alone, it makes sense to hold off on sex until you are in an adult relationship.

There are plenty of other things to consider as well. You'll be ready to have sex when you are able to maturely handle the physical consequences of doing it. That means you are ready to handle the possibility of pregnancy and sexually transmitted diseases (STDs). **Before you have sex, you must be confident and comfortable protecting yourself from pregnancy and from STDs.** And since no birth control is 100 percent effective (except abstinence), you must also be prepared to handle a possible pregnancy, because you could be that one who has a contraceptive failure.

Being prepared for all that requires more than just maturity and communication. It also requires financial stability, meaning a steady flow of money. Not many teens have that, and that's why most teen pregnancies result in a mom and child living in poverty. The brain development issue we mentioned above is why most teen moms end up without having the baby's daddy around for very long. It's not the best way to raise a child, and certainly not what you would hope for yourself, but it happens all the time. Girls who have dreams of college, careers, and stable families are often thrown completely off track by a pregnancy that leaves them as teen mothers struggling to get an education and make enough money to live and provide for their babies.

Last, but just as important, sex carries a huge emotional risk. Once you start having sex, your emotions go into overdrive. Sex is meant to be a private, deep connection between two people who care about each other. When sex becomes casual, or the relationship doesn't feel safe or secure, you can't help but feel it in your gut. It's just the way our brains are wired. Teen boys don't generally think of sex as such an emotional thing. But girls, in particular, have a very hard time separating sex from emotional security and how they feel about themselves. Not only is there self-blame sometimes, but there are also the rumors and name-calling that can start because someone finds out your business. A girl who already feels bad about her relationship may be labeled as a slut. Rumors fly. Her reputation takes a hit. It all hurts emotionally.

If you start having sex before both of you are emotionally, physically, and financially ready, your emotions will pay the price. You will worry yourself to death over a late period, feeling nauseated, noticing a bump in your private parts, or having a sore on your lip. If you're not having sex, those things can't really bother you that much, because you can be certain that you're not pregnant and you haven't caught an STD. We've known many teen girls who have had sex in the past, but stopped because it simply wasn't worth all the stress and worry. Those are smart girls who learned from their mistakes. It can be very liberating to free yourself from the stresses of teen sex.

So if you're trying to decide when it's okay for you, maybe we should summarize with a checklist:

I'll be ready to have sex when (check the ones that you want, but we've already checked a couple of no-brainers for you):

☑ When I have a partner who I trust, love, respect, and with whom I feel safe.

☑ When I have a partner who is committed, responsible, and loves me for who I am.

☑ When I have learned about the ways I can protect myself against unwanted pregnancy, and I am using an effective birth control method that seems best for me.

☑ When I am certain I am protecting myself as best I can against STDs by using condoms correctly and consistently or being in a committed, adult, monogamous relationship where both my partner and I have tested negative for STDs for at least six months.

☐ When I'm engaged or married. (This is an admirable goal. Statistics say you won't make it, but we challenge you to beat the statistics. It is by far the safest and smartest goal for obvious reasons. In a long-term monogamous relationship, you won't have to worry about STDs, and if a pregnancy occurs, even an unplanned one, you are much more prepared to handle it and provide for a child. Your chances of having a stable family are greatly increased.)

☐ When I'm out of college. (This is a realistic and very smart goal. Once you have a college education, your goals for employment and your ability to provide for a child are much greater. Your relationships are more likely to be mature and based on true love and commitment.)

☐ When I'm out of high school. (This is a very realistic goal, but we think you can do better! Once you are out of high school, you have a better chance at getting a job, and you are more likely to continue your education. By then, you are typically dealing with older guys who are slightly more mature about relationships and commitment, but you probably aren't financially stable yet. Once you have reached your late teens, you are likely to have greater self-confidence. You are also more likely to make a decision that is based on your personal code of ethics rather than just hooking up for the thrill of it or to get rid of the pressure from your friends.)

☐ Make up your own. . . .

☐ Oops, I've already had sex, but I think I'm ready to set a new goal for myself. I'm going to hold out until . . .

"How can I let a boy know I'm not interested in sex without losing him as a boyfriend?"

The Full Scoop: If you're in a relationship that's getting serious, you need to be communicating clearly about what matters to you. This is one of the most important conversations you can have with your BF. If you don't feel comfortable talking about sex and your sexual boundaries, you really aren't ready to do it.

If your BF doesn't honor your sexual boundaries or pressures you to have sex when you're not ready, he doesn't care about you as a person because he isn't respecting you. Make sure you give him a chance by explaining why you want to wait before this becomes an issue. If he still puts the pressure on you, you can know for sure that he isn't listening or doesn't care. That means he's not the right guy for you right now. Consider it a red flag.

A guy who really cares about you and your relationship with him will wait for you. You just need to make sure he understands your boundaries. He can't understand them if you don't tell him. Body language (like pushing his hand away) doesn't compute for most guys! **Clear communication with words is key.**

"My BF doesn't want to go beyond kissing, but I'm ready. How do I get him to do more?"

The Full Scoop: Be patient! There will be lots of time for more. **Just like we want guys to respect girls' sexual boundaries, you have to respect theirs.** As your relationship grows in emotional intimacy, he may become more comfortable. But there's nothing wrong with perfecting your kissing skills and not going any further. It's very safe and fun!

"How can I make my parents like my boyfriend?"

The Full Scoop: Instead of asking how you can make your parents like him, you should first be asking, "Why don't they like him?" **You may be so blinded by love that you totally miss seeing certain traits or behaviors that others see as big red**

flags. Maybe they know he's jealous. Maybe they've heard he's a player. Maybe they know his parents are never around to supervise his activities. Maybe they've seen him drinking alcohol at a football game or getting into a fight.

You probably know him best by his adorable smile and the sweet way he hugs you when he sees you. But the things your parents may know are also important. Give them some credit and at least hear them out. If they don't like him just because he has a pierced ear or long hair or grungy clothes, maybe you can educate them about his sweet ways. But if they don't like him for more serious reasons, like the ones we've listed above, you need to listen and recognize that these are red flags and could mean danger for you. Even if you're not ready to call it off because of your parents' opinion, you should at least respect what they've told you and give it some consideration. It might just make you a bit more cautious and aware. After all, your parents just want what's best for you, and they want to make sure you stay safe. That's probably what's behind their concerns.

"What can I do if our whole relationship is about sex?"

Quickie Answer: Change things or get out.

The Full Scoop: This is a big reason we encourage teen girls to wait until they are older to have sex. Teen guys and teen girls see sex very differently. Research has proven how the brain responds to sexual urges in teen males, teen females, and adults. Compared with adult men, **teen guys don't link sex with emotional**

connections and commitment. That means teen guys have sex because it feels good, not because they feel like it is an expression of their love and commitment in a relationship. As they mature and become adults, they begin to understand and express emotions a little better.

Most teen girls and adult women, on the other hand, have sex to strengthen a relationship or to express their feelings of love or for some other complex reason. Teen girls rarely have sex just because it feels good. In fact, when asked, most teen girls don't think sex is all that great physically, but they like making their BF feel good and they like the closeness.

There are certainly exceptions to both of these (like guys who have sex because they are emotionally connected or girls who have sex just for physical pleasure), but in most humans, these differences are consistent, according to the research.

So what does all this mean? It's a good idea to wait, but if you're involved sexually and you feel like the whole relationship revolves around sex, you have a couple of choices. You can tell him you don't like the way the relationship is going and you'd like to spend more time getting to know each other in ways other than having sex. Or you can get out. Learn from it, and make sure your next relationship doesn't end up the same way. Either way, it takes a lot of self-control and communication, but it's a huge step toward building better relationships.

"I would do anything to keep him as my BF. Why am I so obsessed with him?"

Quickie Answer: It's called a "crush" because it crushes your ability to act sensibly.

The Full Scoop: It happens all the time. Some girls will do anything to keep a guy. They'll compromise their val-
ues and standards. They'll have sex when they don't want to. They'll blow
off their friends when they shouldn't. They'll ignore their families when
they need them. They'll drive by their BF's house fifteen times a day just
to see if his car is in the driveway.

When you feel like this about your BF, like you would do anything,
you need to take a deep breath and think about reality. This is the hardest time to remember your values and concentrate on what you really
expect in a relationship, but it's the most important time to do just that.
**Decide now about sexual boundaries, how you will maintain your
friendships, and how you will find time to do the things you enjoy
besides being with him.** Maybe you can include him in some of your
favorite activities or family time so you aren't putting your life on hold
just to be with him. In a healthy relationship, you'll be able to stay true
to yourself, your friends, your family, AND your crush, as long as you
keep your relationship in perspective.

"Why do guys feel they can hook up one day and not talk the next?"

The Full Scoop: We already mentioned that guys don't have the
same emotional connection with sex that girls
do—at least not in their teen years. For some, sex is closer to a recre-
ational sport than an intimate act. When guys have that attitude about
sex, why would they feel the need to "talk" afterward? It's like playing a

game. Once you win, it's over. No need for further discussion unless they're just bragging to their friends.

For girls and women, sex has more of an emotional connection. We're not trying to stereotype, but science supports the fact that teen girls' brains and teen guys' brains respond very differently to sexual arousal and sexual activity. A girl who has sex typically feels a deep, intimate experience with the guy. Her reasons for having sex are complex, but usually include things like building greater intimacy, strengthening the relationship, demonstrating her love, and looking toward a future with her partner. But a teen guy having sex might just do it because it feels good, kind of like scratching an itch.

So, doesn't it make sense to avoid hook-ups? Even though some might try to talk themselves into believing that they're okay with casual sex, it's really difficult for most girls to disconnect sex from their emotions. On a deeper emotional level, though, most people want more than just a casual hook-up, but hook-ups don't provide anything more.

"How come it's cool to be a player but horrible to be a slut?"

Quickie Answer: It's known as the double standard, and it's been around since before your grandparents were born.

The Full Scoop: The double standard means it's okay for guys to have sex, but it's not okay for girls. Even the names emphasize the difference. "Player" sounds cool and fun. "Slut"? "Skank"? "Whore"? No thanks. A guy who has sex with every girl he dates is a player, but a girl who has sex with every guy she dates is a slut. So why is it like that?

It probably comes down to the fact that women carry the burden of the consequences of sex. They are expected to be mature and responsible when it comes to sex because they are the ones who get pregnant or end up infertile from an infection. For men, it's different. They can't get pregnant, and infections have little implication for their reproductive health. So, men not only get away with sex, sex makes them appear strong and manly. Maybe it's a testosterone thing.

The downside for guys is that they are often expected to be "macho" and sexual. They have a lot of social pressure to "get laid." If they don't have sex, they are sometimes considered pansies, or called a wuss or gay. So guys don't necessarily have it easy.

For girls, it's not easy either. In fact, we know girls who have been called sluts but never even had sex. We also know girls who probably live up to the label, but what good does that label offer? As a girl, it's important for you to avoid spreading rumors or ruining someone's reputation. Don't use the word lightly, because it hurts.

"How do I tell my BF it's over?"

The Full Scoop: Nicely. If you're ending a relationship that was good at some point, it was probably built on honest caring and friendship. It will be important to make sure it ends on the same note. You may recognize the end is coming as you start to grow apart and have less in common. **To maintain your own self-respect and to preserve his sense of self, it will be important to be honest and**

respectful. You may just need to explain that you still like him and respect him but that the relationship is no longer, well, you can fill in the blank . . . it's no longer right for you . . . growing . . . fun . . . heading in the direction you hoped for, and so on.

As a teen, your identity is constantly developing, and your preferences will change. That's okay. But sometimes it means you and your BF grow apart. Nothing's wrong with either of you; it's just time to move on. So, if you sense that the relationship needs to end, don't let it get to the point where you are both angry and resentful. End it while you can have a civil conversation and remain friends. And make sure you end it before you outwardly start a new relationship with someone else. You never know. **He may be the best friend you've ever had, but just didn't cut it as your BF.** You may also find that you had fun while it lasted, but you no longer have anything in common. That's alright, too. Just do your best to end it in a way that won't leave him angry.

If the tables are turned and he's ending it with you, it can hurt. You can maintain your dignity by listening to him and trying to be mature about the breakup. It may be for the same reasons we mentioned above, that his preferences and identity are changing. If he tells you something hurtful, like you're too clingy, too controlling, too moody, too unavailable, too much, too little, too anything, don't try to argue. He's already made up his mind. He may even feel the need to use hurtful words to make sure he accomplishes the breakup.

What if he has fallen for someone else? Ouch. It always hurts to be on the dropped end of a breakup, but try to maintain your dignity. Remind yourself that teen relationships usually last no more than three or four months anyway. **You can learn something from every relationship, but**

you can't change someone's feelings for you, no matter how much you cry, grovel, or beg. Don't go there! If you turn the breakup into a major drama, you will also lose respect. Even though you may be hurt, try to find a private place to express your emotions. You can definitely talk with your friends about it, but don't scream it in the halls at school. Teens love a big drama, but don't let your breakup take center stage.

Finally, if you're ending it because of a red flag event, he's obviously got a lot to learn or he's just a total jerk. That's when it might not be such a bad idea to let him know. But be careful. **Guys who raise red flags in relationships can be dangerous. If you need to break up with someone like that, consider your safety first.** You may need to have a friend around or even let him know in the safety of your own home with your parents around. You also want to make sure that a trusted adult is aware of the red flag event so they can help you if the situation gets out of hand.

Ending a relationship will almost always hurt someone's feelings. The good news is that most breakups can help you learn something about yourself that can be useful in future relationships. Try to hold on to the positive things you learn and keep looking up. You might enjoy the time you have being "single" for a while. Get back into your hobbies, your girlfriends, and your family. Try something new. If you keep yourself moving and looking forward, you'll have a lot more fun being you, and you'll have a better chance of noticing when a good guy steps in your direction.

Think It Through

Think It Through

OPTION 2. (how it could have gone differently)

Aidan makes his request

Sydney does NOT do it and assumes Aidan is a ∹ LOSER ∹ for expecting that on a first date

She moves on and finds a truly great guy who likes her for who she is and not for what she will do.

Sydney preserves her self respect

She gains CONFIDENCE in the "dating game"

Think It Through

OPTION 3. (another way it could have gone...)

Aidan makes his request

Sydney tells Aidan that she really likes him & is flattered to be out with him **BUT** that's just <u>not</u> who she is, SO she can't do it.

Aidan respects that and actually has a great time talking with her & getting to know her better

Aidan laughs and tells her to find her own ride home. They never speak to each other again.

Aidan takes her home and calls another girl who will "put out."

Sydney preserves her SELF RESPECT

Sydney doesn't have to waste her time with WORTHLESS, SELFISH guys!

Chapter

"Do I really need to go to the gynecologist?"

Help with what's up "down there"

A Real-Life Dilemma

"**N**onfat mocha latte with double whip cream," Sydney said, sliding into the usual booth at the Brew & Buzz. A waitress with multiple piercings nodded, but didn't bother to write it down. It was what Sydney ordered whenever the girls gathered at the trendy café, a few blocks from Lakeside High.

She waved to a couple of friends, but didn't see Tasha or Chelsea, who were meeting her there. Amanda couldn't make it—something about studying for a French quiz. Honestly? The girl logged more time with her nose in a book than the three of them combined.

Just beginning their junior year, the four of them had been friends since the third grade. A pinky-swear, I'd-let-you-read-my-diary kind of friendship since the day Trey Ramsey tried to get Chelsea to either kiss him or eat dirt behind the dugout. She'd almost opted for the dirt when Tasha had wandered by, followed by Sydney and Amanda. They'd promptly rescued Chelsea from Trey's dirty-nailed clutches. The incident, like any good playground tale, had flourished over the years. And, well, they certainly weren't going to let Chelsea forget it. Without

Sydney, Tasha, and Amanda, she would have ended up a love slave to Trey Ramsey, who now played the tuba and had a disturbing obsession with Japanese comic books. Or so they liked to remind her every time they passed him in the hall. When Sydney finally spotted Chelsea and Tasha, the thought sent her into a fit of laughter.

"What's so funny?" Chelsea asked, her usually perky, cheerleader persona displaying an uncharacteristic scowl. The cheerleader part suited her, blonde and bubbly with a buoyant smile and muscular legs that looked as if they were designed to wear that tiny pleated skirt.

"It's nothing, really." Sydney struggled to keep from laughing. She needed to stop. Chelsea took her fair share of teasing from the girls. The only one who'd made the cheerleading squad, the only one with a steady boyfriend and, oddly, the one who most lacked self-confidence. Go figure. "Hey, why were you guys so late?" she asked, quickly changing gears.

Tasha, who was the star athlete of the group, slid into the booth as Chelsea scrunched in beside her. "We, um, we had to make a pit stop . . . at the pharmacy . . . to get something."

"Shut up," Chelsea snapped, also uncharacteristically.

"To get what?" Sydney demanded, her voice dropping to a secretive hush.

"Something . . . it's nothing. Did you order yet?" Tasha asked, clearly trying to shift the subject.

"Yeah," she said, keeping with the covert whisper. "But pierced-parts AJ is our waitress. It'll be a while, so why don't you confess and tell me what you had to get at the pharmacy?" But just then, AJ reappeared with Sydney's order.

"Ah, I was wonderin' where the rest of the gals were hangin'," the waitress said, placing Sydney's drink in front of her.

To Sydney, AJ was a cultural conversation piece: she'd gone to the Goth side about a year ago, dying her blonde hair the color of midnight and wearing a wardrobe to match. But her spiky haircut did show off an array of stud and bar jewelry in her ears and a diamond in her nose, as well as a tongue ring. Every time Sydney saw the thing, she cautiously rolled her own tongue around her mouth. It just looked like it hurt.

"Too much caffeine at the pep rally?" AJ asked, cocking her chin toward Chelsea, who was wiggling around in her seat as if something had bit her. "Can I get you decaf?"

"Uh, no. I'll just have a Diet Coke," she answered, fiddling with a paper napkin.

"Me too," said Tasha. AJ nodded and headed back to the kitchen.

Sydney's chin dropped to her balled fist, examining her two friends. They were on the bizarre side of quiet. "Okay, what's going on? Give, both of you," she said, glaring at Chelsea, who would naturally be the one to crack. "What's at the pharmacy that's such a super secret?"

Tasha shot a sideways glance at Chelsea, but was clearly keeping quiet.

"Okay, I'll play. Let's see, hair dye . . . tampons, dirty magazines . . ." There was still no reaction from either girl, and Sydney's eyes widened. "Condoms. Ohmigosh! You bought condoms? You and Zach are gonna do it?" she gasped.

"No!" Chelsea insisted. "And keep your voice down. If I were going to buy condoms, why would I take Tasha? Like that wouldn't be way weird."

Sydney leaned back, feeling a little disappointed. It had been among the most tantalizing questions since Chelsea and Zach's summer romance had continued, hot and heavy, into the fall. "Then what?"

"Oh, for . . . can we just not talk about it, please?" she said, fingers weaving through her blonde hair.

"She has an itch," Tasha offered. "A, um, personal itch."

"An itch," Sydney repeated. She sipped her latte, looking as disappointed as she felt. "Big deal."

"Would be if it were your itch," Chelsea said, squirming again in her seat. "Tasha went with me. To help find, you know, like a cream or something—to kill it."

Sydney leaned back into the conversation. "That nasty, huh? You know, I had a yeast infection last spring. It was so bad I wanted to use a hair brush to scratch my . . . never mind. I tried some over-the-counter itch relief stuff . . . didn't work."

"That's what I tried to tell her," said Tasha. "She needs to go to the doctor. I don't see what the big deal is. Just tell your mom . . ."

"I can't!" Chelsea said, tears on the rim of her big green eyes.

"Oh, Chelsea, you're being ridiculous!" Tasha said.

"If I tell my mom I need to see a gynecologist, you know exactly what she's going to think!"

"Well, that's true," Sydney said, slurping her latte and shrugging her shoulders.

"You're not helping," Tasha said.

"Besides, I don't want to go to *that kind* of doctor. It's disgusting. My mom's doctor is about a hundred years old. I'd die on the table before he even . . . even . . ."

"Got the speculum out?" offered Tasha. "Or should I say in?"

"The what?" Chelsea asked with a wide-eyed blink.

"The . . . you know . . . duckbill thing. . . . It's the thingy the doctor uses to look inside your thingy," Sydney offered in a whisper, motioning toward their collective lower halves. "Don't let Tasha scare you. Her mother, the doctor, equipped her with all the right medical terms in creation. She was the only second grader I knew who asked to be excused so she could go urinate."

"Just shut up!" Tasha said, folding her arms in exasperation. "Again, not the point. Listen, Chel. Going to the gynecologist is no biggie. If you had a heart problem, you'd go to a cardiologist, right?"

"I guess so."

"So what's the difference? They're specially trained for that part of the body. It's what they do. Seen one, seen 'em all, I'm sure."

"No big deal for them maybe. But . . ."

"I know what you mean," Sydney said, sucking down the last of her drink. "For me, eventually the itch won out over the fear. And it wasn't that bad. In fact, my doctor was pretty cool. She said that anything we talked about was completely private; she couldn't discuss it with anyone. Even my mom. So if you're thinking about you and Zach, well, you know . . ."

"One thing at time," Tasha said. "If you don't want to see your mom's doctor, and I wouldn't blame you, my mom knows a bunch from the hospital. Lots of them are women. All you have to do is ask."

Chelsea crumpled the napkin, which she'd been mauling since the conversation began. "Okay, Tasha, I'm asking. Like Syd said, anything's better than this."

Doc Talk:
The Way **We See It**

YUCK. Whoever wants to go to a doctor for a problem in the privates? It's okay to feel that way. We're used to it. Our patients may love us, but they hate having to see us for those types of problems.

Well, guess what? Problems can come up with pretty much every part of your body, including "down there." So why not go to a doctor who deals with those parts or "those issues" all the time? As a matter of fact, doctors who regularly deal with the "down there" issues are actually used to teen girls feeling awkward and grossed out about it. But they're also trained to help. They can answer your questions about private things. They can offer confidential care. They can give good health advice. And they can be your favorite person in the world when they fix a problem, especially if you have a problem like Chelsea's.

Now that you are through the puberty stuff, it's important to find a doctor who you trust and can get to when you need help. You need to feel comfortable with his or her medical care (and we'll use "her" whenever we refer to doctors from now on), you are comfortable being honest with her, and you feel like you can discuss anything and everything with her. It also helps if she is someone who puts you at ease.

This chapter will take you through some "hang-ups" on the minds of many teen girls: worries about seeing a gynecologist, questions about their bodies, confusion about periods, and ponderings about other private stuff. You may not have any questions or hang-ups right now at all. But it's likely that you will at some point. Remember that our answers are only a start. Make sure you find a doctor or other healthcare professional who can help you stay informed and healthy. And again, if you have other questions that we haven't covered here, e-mail us through our website (www.girlology.com). We'll keep adding answers there!

YOU Asked!

"When should I see a gynecologist instead of my pediatrician?"

The Full Scoop: It all depends on how you feel about your doctor and what your doctor is addressing with you. A pediatrician is a doctor who specializes in treating children and teenagers. Some pediatricians even specialize in taking care of teens only. They are called adolescent medicine specialists. A gynecologist is a doctor who specializes in women's health, particularly pregnancy and reproductive health issues (like periods, sex, sexually transmitted infections, and problems related to the vagina, ovaries, and the rest of the reproductive tract). Both pediatricians and gynecologists are trained to provide medical care for teen girls, but some doctors are better with teen girls than others. There are lots of doctors who enjoy taking care of teens, actually *like* them, and are in touch with the issues that teens face today—that's the type of doctor you need.

The most important thing in finding a doctor is to make sure you feel like you can communicate honestly and openly. During your teen and early adult years, you will, no doubt, need medical advice, treatment, or at least accurate information on things like relationships, sex, alcohol and drugs, birth control, infections, and general health. So whether you use a pediatrician, a gynecologist (ob-gyn), a family physician, or an adolescent medicine specialist, the most important thing is to find a doctor you trust and can confide in. If you've had the same doctor all your life, you may feel uncomfortable discussing matters related to sex and "growing up" because you feel you are still being treated like a child. Sometimes a different doctor in the same practice may work for you, or even a nurse practitioner or physician's assistant may be the person you feel most comfortable with. Sometimes, you may just want to start with a new doctor. There are a lot of great doctors and other healthcare providers for teens out there.

Once you hit your early teens, your doctor should take time to talk with you alone without your parent or guardian around. She will probably talk with you about your body, sex, drugs, safety, relationships, and sexuality. If you have a male doctor, there may be a nurse or assistant in the room during your discussion and during the exam. If your doctor is trying to talk to you about this stuff with your mom in the room and never insists on spending some time talking with you by yourself, you need to find a doctor who respects your privacy and encourages you to be honest and open with your questions and concerns. **You might not even have any-thing "private" to discuss with your doctor, and you might want your mom to stay with you, but having time alone with your doctor is impor-tant to help you start taking responsibility for your own health.** It's part of growing up and being more independent and responsible.

If you have had sex or are thinking about having sex, it is extra impor-tant to have time alone to ask any questions you have. You need a doctor who will make sure you are on the best birth control method for you, test you for STDs, take a Pap smear when you need it, and discuss STD pre-vention. She will also talk with you realistically about the responsibilities and important considerations involved if you choose to be sexually active.

"How should I tell my mom I want to see a gynecologist?"

The Full Scoop: **Speak up!** Honesty is always the best policy, but you might be afraid that your parents will totally freak out and assume you are having sex because you ask to see a gynecologist. Some parents will do exactly that, and some moms will understand. Start out by saying something reassuring like, "I don't want you to think the wrong thing, but I'd like to make an appointment with a gynecologist." When she asks why, you can have several reasons, such as "I feel like I'm treated like a baby at my other doctor's office." "I have some questions about my period." "I just think it's time I had a more grown-up doctor. My friend goes to one she really feels comfortable with." "I'm tired of sitting in the waiting room with the Barney wallpa-per and the toy trucks." "I'm thinking about becoming sexually active, and I'd like to learn more about birth control." "My cramps are getting worse and the medicine you got me isn't helping anymore." "I had sex and I'm scared." Whoa! Could you ever really say that to your mom?

We hope you could discuss anything with your mom, but we know a lot of girls who don't feel that way. Sometimes, though, you just need to give her a little more credit for being able to handle it and help you. You've heard the phrase "better safe than sorry," right? Most parents of teens begin to realize the importance of that phrase as their children enter the teenage years. They expect you to behave a certain way, but they also know that accidents happen and teens take risks that parents don't like. If you tell your mom you need to see a gynecologist, most moms will help you get there, so give honesty a try.

If you absolutely can't be honest with your parents because you might get seriously injured or you are scared for your safety, you can get to a gynecologist or other reproductive health professional without your parents' permission. Free medical care is available in most cities through your county health department. You can find the health departments listed in the government section of your phone book. You could also ask your school guidance counselor or any doctor's office for the number or address.

"What exactly is a pelvic exam?"

The Full Scoop: First of all, let us reassure you that **just because you go to a gynecologist doesn't necessarily mean you get a pelvic exam.** A pelvic exam is obviously an exam of the pelvis. That includes the vulva, anus, vagina, cervix, uterus, and ovaries. In girls who aren't having any problems, it's only necessary when you become twenty-one years old or sexually active, whichever comes *first*. Sometimes a pelvic exam may be necessary in younger girls who are not sexually active if there is a problem, like pelvic pain, abnormal discharge, irregular menstrual bleeding, or some other symptom that could signal an abnormality.

A pelvic exam starts with you lying down on your back on the exam table. You'll have a sheet over your lap and legs to help you feel a little more covered. Your feet are put in the stirrups (they're foot holders that stick out from the table). Then you have to bend your knees to slide your butt to the very edge of the exam table. It's an awkward position because your legs are spread a little, your feet are in the stirrups, and your butt feels like it's hanging off the edge of the table. To top that off, your doctor will sit at the end of the table between your legs to look at your vulva and examine your vagina. Embarrassing? Most girls and women feel embarrassed or awkward, but you need to remember that doctors, especially gynecologists, do this all the time and **it's just another part of your body that needs to be checked.** May sound pretty gross, but it's not that different from looking up your nose—just a bit more personal.

Once your doctor examines the vulva and labia by looking at it, she will use something called a speculum to look inside your vagina. The speculum is either metal or plastic with a handle and two blunt, curved "blades" that look like a narrow duck bill and can be opened by a lever on the handle. The good news is that there are different-sized speculums. The size most doctors would use on a teenager is about the width and length of a super tampon . . . no bigger. There are larger ones and smaller ones that are used in different circumstances, but you can definitely ask to see the speculum before your doctor uses it. If you've ever had sex, it might be reassuring to know that the speculum is definitely smaller than an erect penis.

Your doctor will gently slide the speculum into your vagina and then open the blades a little so she can see your cervix at the end of your vagina. The sensation is uncomfortable, but shouldn't be painful. The whole process is much more comfortable if you can keep your butt and vaginal muscles relaxed. If you tense up down there, you're squeezing against metal or hard plastic, and it will hurt more. The sensation is not that different from when the doctor has to look in your ears . . . uncomfortable but not really painful.

If you have ever had sex, your doctor will probably use a cotton swab to take some of the mucus from your cervix to test for chlamydia and gonorrhea. She'll use another swab to take a sample of your vaginal discharge to inspect under a microscope for infections. If you need a Pap smear (see next question), she will also take that by twirling a soft brush inside your cervix to collect cells. The brush is then swirled in a liquid and sent to the lab to be tested. This sounds like a lot, but in reality, the speculum is in your vagina no longer than a minute.

Once the speculum comes out, it's time for the internal exam. The internal exam is important because it's how your doctor can feel your uterus and ovaries to make sure they're normal. She'll probably stand up for this part and put some lubricant (jellylike, slippery liquid) on her fingers (she'll be wearing gloves!). She'll gently insert one or two fingers into your vagina. The other hand will be placed on your lower abdomen over your bladder and uterus. She'll feel your uterus and ovaries between her hands to note the size and shape of them. This is how ovarian cysts are diagnosed and it's also how we find out if your uterus is a normal size (it will be larger in pregnancy) or if it's tender (which can happen with infection or with other problems).

Occasionally, your doctor may need to do a rectal exam if she finds an abnormality, but usually, a rectal exam is not necessary in teens. If it's done, your doctor will insert one finger into the anus to feel the inside of the rectum and the structures around it. It doesn't hurt, but it makes you feel like you have to poop. Don't worry, you won't.

Gee . . . sounds wonderful, huh? **Honestly, it's not that big of a deal.** Most girls walk away from their first pelvic exam saying, "It really wasn't as bad as I thought it was going to be." Just remember that it's a normal part of any checkup for girls who are sexually active and for all women over twenty-one. Your doctor certainly won't consider it a big deal, and you can be reassured to know that your girl parts are no different from all the other girl parts they see every day!

"What's a Pap smear?"

Quickie Answer: A test for cervical cancer.

The Full Scoop: The Pap smear is named for the man who invented it, Dr. Papanicolaou. "Pap" is much easier to say! **The Pap smear may be part of a pelvic exam, but it's not the only reason for a pelvic exam, and sometimes it's not even done during a pelvic exam.**

Taking a Pap smear involves scraping some cells off of the cervix and just inside the cervical canal (which is the pathway up the cervix that leads into the uterus). "Scrape" sounds worse than it is. Have you ever looked at your cheek cells under a microscope in biology class? If you have, you probably got them by rubbing a Q-tip on the inside of your cheek. Taking a Pap smear is not much different from that except the cells are taken from the cervix instead of inside the mouth. Once the cells are scraped off, they are placed in a special liquid and then put on a microscope slide where they are stained. Under a microscope, abnormal cells may signal precancer or cancer of the cervix.

The good news is that cervical cancer usually grows slowly. Catching it in the early, precancer stages allows doctors to remove the abnormal cells through a minor surgical procedure usually done in the office. Removing the abnormal cells can prevent cancer from developing. Pap smears have been very effective in decreasing the number of women who die from cervical cancer because we have been able to treat them early.

You should have your first Pap smear within three years of when you first have sex or by the time you are twenty-one years old (whichever comes *first!*). To get a Pap smear, you will need a pelvic exam. BUT, having a pelvic exam doesn't necessarily mean you had a Pap smear. A lot of girls and women get confused about that and think that they've had a Pap if they had an examination with a speculum. Not true.

Now you know the facts. If you've had a pelvic exam, you should ask your doctor exactly what tests were done. It's important to be smart about your health and know what your doctors are doing for you.

"Will I get confidential care at the gynecologist's office?"

Quickie Answer: Yes, but . . .

The Full Scoop: At any doctor's office, you have the right to confidential care, even as a teenager. That means anything you discuss in private with your doctor or nurse must be kept private unless the doctor or nurse has your permission to discuss it with your parent. Even if you are under eighteen and considered a minor, in most states you have the right to consent to your own treatment if it involves pregnancy, STDs, or substance abuse. BUT (you knew there was a *but* to this, huh?) there are some things that may not always be kept confidential.

* If something you discuss indicates that you are a danger to yourself or someone else, your doctor is obligated to tell your parents or guardian. That means if you are threatening to kill or seriously hurt yourself or someone else, your doctor has to tell your parents and possibly other legal officials. Another thing that can be considered suicidal is having unprotected sex with multiple partners. Suicidal? Yep. Because having unprotected sex with multiple partners is basically asking for HIV/AIDS (human immunodeficiency virus), which will eventually lead to death. Behavior like that is actually considered reckless, even suicidal, and many girls have been there, done that.

* Even though what you discuss is kept confidential, if your health care is paid by your parent's insurance, your parents may get a copy of the bill. The insurance bill may list your diagnosis and any tests that were done. That means if you are tested for pregnancy or STDs, your parents may find out indirectly because they can figure it out from the bill. To avoid that, you would need to arrange to pay for your visit in cash or with a credit card and ask that insurance not be billed. Talk about expensive! Obviously, this isn't doable for a lot of girls. It's one more reason that honesty is the best policy. If your parents know exactly why you are seeing

your doctor, they won't be surprised when the insurance statement arrives. To avoid this, your other option would be to go to a free medical clinic like we mentioned before.

✻ If you are under eighteen, your parents can always request a copy of your medical records. So essentially, they can legally access information about you from your doctor's office. As physicians, we can say (fortunately!) that it is extremely rare for parents to go to that extreme. Most parents honor the confidentiality of the doctor/patient relationship because they recognize that doctors are there to promote health and safety.

Confidentiality is a very important part of your relationship with your doctor. If you can't be honest with your doctor because you fear your parents will know everything you discuss, your doctor can't take care of you and give you the advice and information you need. **All of the specialties in medicine recognize the importance of confidentiality and have rules that require doctors to make every effort to protect your private information.** That should give you some reassurance that your doctor is on your side when it comes to confidentiality.

"Can I go on birth control without my mom finding out?"

Quickie Answer: Yes, but it's a burden on you.

The Full Scoop: Yes, in most states you can get birth control without your parents finding out. You can go to your private doctor or your local health department to get samples and a prescription for birth control without your parents' permission or knowledge. BUT (here it comes again), it is really hard to keep it a secret for long, and it's a burden to have to do so. It's a pain to keep your pills hidden or to sneak to the doctor's office every three months for your birth control shot. It's also a pain to find a way to pay for your birth control without insurance helping or without your parents pitching in. Finally, if you are on hormonal birth control, it is a medication that your other physicians need to know about because some medicines can interfere with birth control. There are also side effects and complications that can result from some birth control methods. So even though you CAN keep it a secret, we recommend that you don't. It's easier to be honest up front than deceptive and secretive until there's a blowup when your secret is discovered. Learn more about birth control in Chapter 7.

"Can a doctor tell if I'm a virgin by looking at my hymen?"

Quickie Answer: Not always.

The Full Scoop: Believe it or not, we occasionally get a parent in our office who asks us to examine their daughter to see if she is still a virgin. Our answer to that is, "Why don't you just ask her?" There are plenty of reasons most responsible doctors do not do "virginity checks." The main reason, though, is that even a trained doctor looking at a hymen can't always tell if a girl has had sex or not. The best way to find out is to have an honest conversation about sexual behaviors.

If you're hoping to hide the fact that you have had sex from your

doctor, that's a huge problem. Either you don't trust your doctor (and you should immediately find one you do trust), or you are in major denial and aren't taking care of your body. It's really important for your doctor to know whether you have ever had sex or even attempted to have sex. Keep reading and you'll understand why.

"Can tampons tear your hymen?"

Quickie Answer: Possibly, but not normally.

The Full Scoop: When you insert a tampon into your vagina, you will do it in a way that is not painful. If you push a tampon in the wrong direction or too quickly into your vagina, it will cause pain and you'll stop. That pain is usually coming from the hymen. The hymen can be pretty sensitive and it will hurt if you're not being gentle, but it also stretches as pressure is applied to it. Most girls don't inflict pain on themselves with tampon insertion, so most girls do not tear their hymen by using tampons, even the super-plus tampons.

There is one exception we should mention, though. Some girls who are born with a hymen that has a particularly small hole in the center will not be able to use tampons easily. If you have tried and tried to get a tampon into your vagina, but it just seems too painful or difficult, you should see a doctor. Sometimes a small cut can be made (after applying numbing cream so you don't feel it!) in the hymen to enlarge the hole so a tampon can be inserted.

"What exactly is 'popping the cherry'"?

The Full Scoop: Popping the cherry is a slang phrase that is used to imply "tearing the hymen" by having sex. It's a pretty derogatory phrase that makes sex just seem like a game or sport. It's definitely a term that is disrespectful to girls and women.

"How much discharge is normal?"

The Full Scoop: We're so glad you asked, because that's a question that lingers in the minds of a lot of girls and women, but it's just not something that comes up in casual conversation. If you haven't heard, let us be the first to reassure you that vaginal discharge usually shows up around puberty, and all girls and women have it. Why? It's actually the way the vagina cleanses itself and stays moist and comfortable.

Vaginal discharge is the creamy, clear-to-white-to-yellow stuff that oozes out of your vagina. After it dries in your underwear, it might look yellow and become a little crusty (okay, you can say ewww). It's usually enough to lightly stain the crotch of your underwear, so, yes, that's normal too. Before your periods ever start, you may have discharge every day. It should be about the same amount on most days.

Once your periods start, the amount of discharge will increase or decrease depending on where you are in your menstrual cycle. Sometimes, there's not much discharge at all. Sometimes there's a lot. Sometimes it's thick and yellowish, and sometimes it's thinner and clear—almost like egg whites. It is totally normal to have it. It may have a slight odor, but it isn't stinky. It shouldn't itch or burn your skin. And it shouldn't be green or lumpy. If you pay attention, you'll even begin to notice when it is heavier and when it is thinner. Once you get used to your normal discharge, you'll know when something's not right about it . . . like the smell, the color, or the amount. If you notice a significant change in your "normal" discharge, you should see your doctor to make sure you don't have an infection or other condition that may need to be treated.

A lot of girls think that they will know if they have an infection by the way their discharge looks. For yeast infections, that is sometimes true, but **for sexually transmitted infections, there may be no change in your discharge at all and, in fact, no symptoms at all.** So you can't depend on your discharge to "signal" when you have an STD. The only way to know for sure if you have an infection is to be tested by your doctor or nurse. Of course, if you aren't having sex . . . vaginal, oral, or anal . . . then you won't have to worry about sexually transmitted infections at all. For more information on STDs, see Chapter 8.

"What's that smell?"

The Full Scoop: Some girls worry that they have an odor that comes from their vaginal area. Some think it's there all the time and some only notice it around their period. We can assure you that all discharge has an odor, but it's not a stinky odor or even a very noticeable odor—except perhaps to you. You know how armpits have characteristic odors? Your vagina can have a characteristic odor, too. All these odors start with puberty, and they come from sweat, normal bacteria on the skin, and an increase in oils from certain glands that are only in the armpits and genital area. The good news is that ALL those characteristic odors can be controlled by good hygiene. That means washing regularly—with soap.

In the vagina, there are normal bacteria that can produce a fishy odor under certain circumstances. Want the real scientific scoop? Since you asked . . . a lot of it has to do with acids and bases—like in chemistry. The vagina usually has a pH that is in the acid range. When the vagina is exposed to things that are alkaline (the opposite of acid), it increases the odor created by those bacteria. What things are alkaline? Blood, for one. So when you are on your period, there can be a stronger odor than usual. Soap is alkaline, and you may notice a stronger odor during your shower. Finally, semen is also alkaline, so sex (without a condom) can increase the fishy odor of the vaginal area.

There is also a condition called bacterial vaginosis (or BV) that has, as one of its symptoms, a characteristically fishy odor. The diagnosis is made by looking at the vaginal discharge under a microscope and seeing the responsible bacteria. The bacteria that cause BV also cause the vaginal pH to be much more alkaline than usual. And as we mentioned above, that alkaline pH is related to the fishy odor. BV can be an embarrassing condition because nobody wants a stinky vagina. Fortunately, the diagnosis and treatment are simple, but it requires a prescription medication.

Finally, BV is not considered a sexually transmitted infection. It can occur in girls who have never had sex, but girls who have had sex are much more likely to have it. It is not contagious. In fact, guys can't even get it, but having sex with a guy can play a part in your developing it.

It's important to be treated if you have BV because it increases the risk for other infections. Girls with BV have a higher risk of catching STDs if they are sexually active. That means BV increases the risk for getting HIV and pelvic inflammatory disease (PID). It has also been related to infections inside the uterus and to problems in pregnancy such as preterm birth.

"Is it OK to shave my pubic/vaginal hairs?"

Quickie Answer: Shave some, trim the rest.

The Full Scoop: Hairs around the vagina are there for a reason (and you wanna know that reason, don't you? We'll get to it), but we all agree that hairs on the mons (that's the fatty mound over your pubic bone where your hair grows in the shape of a triangle) can get a bit out of control. They can get long or grow out of bounds. For hair gone wild, it's never a problem to do a little bush trimming. But we mean TRIM, not remove entirely.

For most of the hair on the mons, it's up to you. We recommend trimming with scissors rather than shaving because shaving such coarse hair can lead to some bad ingrown hairs and infected follicles. The biggest complaints about mons hair are usually related to it getting long and bushy. Trimming it down to a shorter length will take care of that problem. For those pesky pubic hairs that poke out from under your bathing suit or underwear lines, **getting rid of them is often necessary for your peace of mind and sense of style.**

There are many methods out there for the job. Do some research before you choose your hair weapon—razors, tweezing, waxing, cream hair removers, and the more permanent options like laser or other intense light treatments are all acceptable options. Some are cheap and easy, while others are time-consuming and expensive, but they can all be pretty uncomfortable. You might need to try a few different methods to find the one that works best for you. Just make sure you carefully follow the directions and precautions that are provided with your method of choice.

If you decide to use a razor (and that's the most common method used by teen girls), you should at least make sure you know the right way to shave hair . . . that's any hair—on your head, in your armpits, on your legs, and on the mons. The area should be cleaned thoroughly with warm soap and water first. That will reduce the bacteria on the skin that could cause infected bumps and keep the hair softer. You should also use a clean, new razor (especially if you're shaving pubic hairs) because of the risk of follicle infections and "razor rash" in this sensitive area. (And never, EVER use someone else's razor.) Make sure you use shaving cream or soapy water first, and then shave the hair in the same direction that it grows. That means you look at the hairs to see if they are growing downward, sideways, whatever. It doesn't guarantee that you'll never get an ingrown hair or infected follicle, but it will reduce the chances.

Ingrown hairs happen when the hair is shaved below the surface of the skin. When it begins to grow back, it curls around and starts to grow into the skin instead of outside the follicle. It can cause a large red bump that also becomes infected or very irritated. Ingrown hairs will usually go away on their own in time, but if they become large and very tender, you may need to see your doctor. We see these all the time in the out-of-bounds hair. So be careful!

For the hairs around the vaginal opening, we have to say PUHLEEEZE don't shave them, and we'll give you a couple of reasons why you shouldn't:

Reason #1: The hairs around the vaginal opening help to pull your vaginal discharge away from the sensitive skin on your vulva. If the discharge stays on that skin (because there's no hair for it to hang on to), it can cause skin irritation bad enough to make you need to see a doctor (we know; we see girls and women with this problem). The reason discharge irritates your skin goes back to that acid/base chemistry thing. Your skin likes things that are pH neutral, but remember, normal discharge has an acid pH—not good for skin. If you shave your vaginal region and then add a thong that rubs that skin between your vagina and your anus, you are setting yourself up for some potentially major irritation! If it happens, the best treatment is to use a skin ointment that contains zinc oxide on the area and let the hair grow back.

Reason #2: It's tough to get a good visual down there. That makes it very easy to nick yourself using a razor or even scissors. Ever had a cut "down there"? Ouch! Band-Aids won't stick, it can be very uncomfortable, and your pee will burn it badly until it heals. Furthermore, there's that ingrown hair thing again. Painful bumps and infected things in the vaginal area are always frightening, not to mention uncomfortable!

"What is a yeast infection and what causes it?"

The Full Scoop: Yeast infections are common "infections" that affect the vagina. You don't get them from coming in contact with germs; you get them because the natural balance of bacteria in the vagina gets out of whack. Bacteria in the vagina? Yep, it's normal. Your skin, your mouth, your intestines, and your vagina all have "healthy" bacteria living in and on them. The healthy bacteria protect them from "bad" bacteria and other organisms. One of the organisms that the normal bacteria keep under control is yeast.

Yeast is a fungus that can cause different types of infections in different body parts. For example, a yeast infection in the mouth is called thrush and a yeast infection between your toes or on your feet is called athlete's foot . . . and a yeast infection on a guy's groin and scrotum is called jock itch. So all yeast infections aren't vaginal infections, but for girls, it's the one that give us the most annoying symptoms—itching and irritation!

A vaginal yeast infection can itch so badly that it makes you want to use a hair brush to scratch down there. Yikes. Besides the itch, it will also change the amount and thickness of your discharge. Usually, it turns thick, clumpy, and sometimes even a greenish or gray color. The loveliest description of the change in discharge that occurs with a yeast infection is "cottage cheesy." Ewwww. Sounds gross, but if it happens to you, it's serious business because you'll want to get relief ASAP! Read on for more information about treating it.

"Can yeast infections go away without treatment?"

Quickie Answer: **Not usually.**

The Full Scoop: Once a yeast infection causes symptoms bad enough to bother you, there is such an abundance of yeast that it is rare for it to go away on its own. Instead, it will typically require using a pill you swallow or a medication (cream, tablets, or

Yogurt can cure a yeast infection.

FALSE. Yogurt, even with live lactobacillus cultures, will not make a yeast infection go away. Some women swear that eating it regularly helps them keep yeast infections away, but there's really no science to prove that's true. And if you already have the symptoms of a yeast infection, neither eating it nor putting it in your vagina will cure you. There are some herbal treatments, like tea tree oil, that some people use, but those typically just relieve some of the annoying symptoms, and the infection itself is not fully cured. Other over-the-counter vaginal itch creams won't do any good either. They just relieve the itching for a little while, but it comes back when the cream wears off, and the yeast is still there to keep you itching and uncomfortable.

ovules) that you insert into the vagina for anywhere from one to seven days (depending on the strength of the medication). Thankfully, yeast infection treatments are available without a prescription, **but if you've never had one, you should always see a doctor first to make sure that's really what it is.** There are other infections and conditions that can cause the same symptoms, but the yeast medications won't cure the other types of infections, so your first treatment should always be directed by a doctor. If you've had a yeast infection before and you are certain that the symptoms are exactly the same, you can try one of the nonprescription medications first. If your discomfort isn't improving within a couple days, or gone within about five days, you should see a doctor.

"If I itch, is it always yeast?"

Quickie Answer: **Absolutely not!**

The Full Scoop: Itching on the vulva and in the vaginal area can be things other than yeast, especially in teens. Just like the rest of the skin on your body can itch for lots of reasons, it's the same "down there." Sometimes, the things that come in contact with the vulva or vaginal area can be the culprit. That includes simple things like detergents, soaps, clothing, and deodorized pads. There are several skin conditions (like dry skin, eczema, psoriasis, and something called lichen sclerosis) that can sometimes cause severe itching or burning. These conditions are treatable, but yeast medications won't help them. They usually require other prescription creams from a doctor.

What's more important to know is that **there are also sexually transmitted infections that can create discharge or skin changes that itch.** So if you've ever had sex, even oral sex, and you have an itchy or burning vagina that is only getting worse, or doesn't get any better after using an over-the-counter yeast medication, then it's definitely time to seek medical attention. You'll need an accurate diagnosis based on tests that are done in a medical setting.

"How common are ovarian cysts?"

Quickie Answer: **Very common.**

The Full Scoop: Did you know that you actually get an ovarian cyst every time you ovulate? True! So, ovarian cysts are very common, but usually not problematic. Every month, as your ovaries prepare to ovulate, a cyst containing the egg will form and enlarge to almost an inch in diameter. Once the cyst reaches that size and the hormones are right, the egg pops out of the cyst—that's ovulation. So, really, you get an ovarian cyst about every month. So what's the big deal about ovarian cysts? The cysts that you hear about causing pain or requiring surgery are usually cysts caused by things other than ovulation. There are many different types, and most of the cysts that occur in teens are benign (that means they are not caused by cancer).

Some cysts don't cause any symptoms, and some may cause pain or a feeling of pressure in the pelvis. The diagnosis is usually made by a physical examination and/or an ultrasound. The ultrasound is a painless test. It's the same thing doctors use when they are looking at a fetus during prenatal care for a pregnant woman. With ovarian cysts, though, sometimes it's too hard to see the cyst when looking through your abdomen, so the ultrasound is done through the vagina.

No fear. To do a vaginal ultrasound, the doctor or ultrasound technician will gently place a long, thin ultrasound probe just inside the vagina. The probe is not much larger than a tampon, so it really isn't a big deal. It allows your doctor to see your ovaries much better and make a more accurate diagnosis. Most of the time, ovarian cysts in teens can be observed. Sometimes a doctor may use birth control pills to "treat" the cyst (they actually help prevent new cysts from forming while the "old" cyst is going away). Occasionally, the way the cyst looks can lead the doctor to do surgery rather than wait and watch. Again, most ovarian cysts in teens are not cancer and they usually go away on their own without surgery.

"I'm fifteen and I haven't started my period. What's wrong?"

Quickie Answer: **Probably nothing, but it's important to pay attention to some details.**

The Full Scoop: There may not be anything wrong because it's normal for girls to start their periods any time between the ages of nine and sixteen. For girls who are "late" starters, though, it can seem like you're the only one of your friends who hasn't reached that point. It may be reassuring to know that the changes that take place from the start of puberty until you start your period are pretty predictable for most girls. If you have breasts and pubic hair, and you are still growing taller, you can relax for now. If you can remember when you started growing breasts, you can depend on your period starting as late as three years after that time.

The other physical change you'll see before you start your period is a big jump in your height. Some girls will grow up to three inches about a year before they start their period. The time of fastest growth happens around six months before you start your period, then your growth slows down. Unless you are measuring your height monthly, it's hard to notice these changes, but sometimes you can just tell it from your clothes.

If you are past the three-year mark from breast development; if you seemed to start into puberty, but it all came to a screeching halt somewhere; or if you are approaching sixteen and still haven't started, you will need to see your doctor or a doctor who specializes in pubertal and hormonal problems. Your pediatrician, family doctor, or an ob-gyn can usually start the evaluation and send you to a specialist if that's needed.

"My periods aren't predictable. Will they ever be?"

Periods can seem totally crazy and unpredictable, especially in the first year or two that you have them. For most girls, they do become fairly predictable, but it might just take some time. If fact, research has shown that the younger you are when you start your periods, the faster they become regular. That doesn't seem fair, but it's true. If you start before age eleven, it typically takes about one year before they become predictable. If you start between eleven and twelve, it takes about three years, and if you start after age twelve (the average age is about twelve and a half), it may take four to eight years or more before you can accurately predict your periods.

So what do you do in the meantime? Well, the good news is that even though you may not have a period cycle that is exactly 28–30 days, you should have your periods somewhere between 21–45 days apart. That's considered normal for girls in the first few years of menstruation. That means you might have a period September 1, then another one September 25 (24 days), then October 31 (36 days), then November 24 (24 days), then January 7 (44 days!). There's no rhyme or reason to that pattern, but those cycle lengths varying from 24–44 days are considered normal.

Some girls will be lucky and have their period every 30 days like clockwork, but that's not the norm. What normally happens is that you will start to establish a fairly regular cycle that may be 3 to 5 days more or less than your average cycle length. Some girls establish their "normal" pattern earlier than others, but most will have their own predictable pattern by age nineteen or twenty.

The best way to predict your periods is to keep them marked on a calendar, and then calculate the cycle length, which is the number of days from the first day of one period to the first day of the next. If you are "regular" you will notice that your cycles are all within 3 to 5 days of the average cycle length. Hmmmmm, let's do the math:

Here's a sample:

FIRST DAY OF PERIOD	CYCLE LENGTH
January 1	
February 4	34
March 5	30
April 1	27
May 3	32
June 5	33
The average cycle length is 34 + 30 + 27 + 32 + 33 = 156; 156/5 = 31.2.	

With an average cycle length of about 31 days, all the cycles are within 4 days (4 more or 4 less) of the average, so that is considered regular. We know. It's not as regular as the TV schedule or even as the garbage pickup day, but it's as regular as the body gets when it comes to periods. This may help you be a bit more prepared for those little surprises.

If you are consistently having periods that are more than forty-five days apart or if you, even once, go more than ninety days without a period, you should see your doctor. It might be an early sign of something called polycystic ovarian syndrome, or it might be some other medical condition that can affect your hormones and your general health. Hormones, and thus periods, are very sensitive to health issues such as body weight changes, medications, thyroid problems, and other endocrine diseases or chronic conditions. It's always good to make sure nothing else is wrong so you can relax about your periods. Oh, and obviously, if you are sexually active and you skip a period, pregnancy is the most common reason for that, so checking in with your doctor is extremely important if you've decided to have sex.

"Is it OK to skip a period occasionally?"

Quickie Answer: Depends . . .

The Full Scoop: Skipping periods can have very serious implications or may be nothing at all. Want the serious implications first? Skipping a period may be the first sign of pregnancy. **If you've had sex and you skip a period, it's time to get serious about finding out why.** If you're pregnant, you've got a lot to think about. If you're not pregnant, you'll understand the fear and worry that is inevitable when you are having sex, even if you are being careful with birth control. You know that birth control is not 100 percent effective (if you don't know, read Chapter 7), so that makes a late period a seriously scary issue. Some girls stop having sex because of this type of scare. They decide that the sex is not worth the worry and stress in their teen years. Wise choice.

If you're not having sex and you skip a period, it can still be serious, but usually it's nothing to worry about. The most common reason for a skipped period is something called anovulation. It means that ovulation doesn't happen. And if you don't ovulate, you don't have a "normal" period. Interestingly, many girls and women will have one, maybe two cycles per year when they do not ovulate. If you don't ovulate, your period will usually be very late or won't happen at all until the next cycle. It might sound like a good thing to get to skip a few periods, but skipping more than a couple of periods can signal health problems and can increase your risk for future health problems.

There are lots of things that can cause anovulation. In your younger teen years, anovulation is more common than in the adult years. That's because your body and hormones are still maturing. The communication between your brain and ovaries is still developing and the signals are not always on time. That's why it may take several years for periods to become "regular" after you first start. So sometimes it's just a maturity issue in the body.

Other causes for anovulation (and skipped or absent periods) include the following:

- Thyroid disease (your thyroid is a gland that affects your metabolism) • A hormonal imbalance (your body may have too much testosterone) • A benign (not cancerous) pituitary tumor (a gland in the brain that produces several important hormones)
- A benign or cancerous tumor of the ovary or adrenal gland
- Excessive weight gain or weight loss • Abnormally low body fat (usually related to anorexia or excessive exercise) • Other chronic diseases like diabetes, obesity, inflammatory bowel disease, cancers, Cushing's disease, premature ovarian failure, and adrenal hyperplasia
- Medications, including antidepressants, antiseizure medications, birth control pills, thyroid medication, steroids, and chemotherapy
- Illicit drugs • Stress!

These sound serious! The important thing to remember is if you skip your period for more than three months, you need to see your doctor to make sure none of the things listed above are to blame.

"Is it OK to get my period more than once a month?"

Quickie Answer: Yes, if it's been at least 21 days since your last period started.

The Full Scoop: The normal length of a menstrual cycle is anywhere from 21 to 45 days. Since a month is about 30 days, you can certainly have two periods in one month if you have a short cycle.

The most common reasons for this include infection or side effects from hormonal birth control methods. There are other less-common, but serious conditions that can also cause frequent, irregular bleeding. If you experience this, it's important to see your doctor to find out why and get it fixed.

"What's the best treatment for cramps?"

The Full Scoop: There are lots of options for alleviating menstrual cramps. The easiest and cheapest way is to try getting regular exercise. Yep, go for a brisk walk or jog. If that's not doing the trick, try placing a heating pad over your lower abdomen (if you don't have a heating pad, fill a clean kneesock with rice, tie the end in a knot to keep the rice from spilling out, and heat it in the microwave for about two minutes). Ahhhhh! If that still isn't helping, you might want to try an over-the-counter nonsteroidal pain medication such as ibuprofen (Motrin, Advil) or naproxen (Aleve, Naprosyn). There are other over-the-counter medications specifically marketed for menstrual cramps, but many of them contain aspirin, which isn't as helpful, and some even contain caffeine, which isn't necessary or helpful for treating cramps.

If the over-the-counter products aren't helping, it's time to have a chat with your mother and/or doctor. For most girls and women, prescription strengths of ibuprofen or naproxen will work well. For other girls, birth control pills may be helpful.

It would be nice if "birth control pills" were called something else for cases like this. They could be called something like "hormonal help" or "period fixers" because those are more descriptive terms. Many girls who have never been sexually active and aren't planning on it anytime soon need to use birth control pills for reasons that have nothing to do with preventing pregnancy. For girls who have menstrual cramps that aren't relieved with pain medicines, birth control pills will successfully treat most of them.

Rarely, there are teens who continue to have cramps that are not controlled with the medications mentioned above. Some of them will need stronger hormonal treatments and some will require surgery to help figure out the cause. If you are in this category, you should be in close contact with your doctor to determine the best treatment for you.

"Why do I get bloated during my period?"

Quickie Answer: Hormones.

The Full Scoop: Okay, you probably don't really want us to go into the details of why this happens. It has to do with your hormonal changes and the effects of those hormones on the way your body retains water and salt. Enough? You probably just want to know how to make it go away.

You can help reduce the swelling and bloating that occurs before or during your period by avoiding salt and salty foods (anything in a can, including drinks, is high in salt unless it says low sodium), exercising, and drinking plenty of water. Some girls will try herbal diuretic tea or over-the-counter diuretics. Although it sounds wrong, you should try to avoid the diuretics (things that make you pee a lot) and drink more water. It can help you "flush out" some of the hormones and salts that are making you bloated.

"When will my boobs finish growing?"

Quickie Answer: (We prefer to call them breasts.) By age 17 or 18, you should be done, but . . .

The Full Scoop: There are a lot of things that affect breast growth. From puberty on, your breasts will grow and change shape until you reach 17 or 18. Now that doesn't mean your breasts will always look like they do when you're 18, because a lot of other things will affect their shape and size, particularly pregnancy and weight changes.

"Is there anything that will make my boobs grow?"

The Full Scoop: Weight gain and pregnancy are the most common reasons for breast growth after your teen years. Losing weight will also affect your breast size. Birth control pills will increase breast size a little for some girls, but once you stop the

Certain pills or exercises will effectively increase your breast size.

FALSE, FALSE, FALSE, FALSE.
The pills are usually loaded with carbohydrates that cause you to gain weight all over, not just in your breasts. What about the exercises? They don't help either. Breasts are made of mostly fat and glandular material, not muscle. Exercises and weight lifting can increase the size of your pectoral muscles that are beneath your breasts, but your breast size won't change.

pill, your breast size returns to normal.

The only way to increase breast size or shape is through plastic surgery. Too many teen girls are worried about their breast size and think plastic surgery is the answer for all their problems. NOT!

If you are uncomfortable with your breast size, bras can often make things better by adding some padding or pushing your breast tissue up and together to enhance what you have. A new bra is a lot easier than surgery.

"My boobs are huge and make my back hurt because they are so heavy. What should I do?"

The Full Scoop: So many girls talk about how they wish they had large breasts, but for girls who really do have large breasts, we know it can be a real problem in several ways. Large breasts make it difficult to find clothes that fit well, affect your comfort in exercise, and can even cause back pain from the weight of carrying them around. Bras can also cause shoulder pain and dents because of the weight held by the straps. And that doesn't even touch on the emotional impact from teasing and self-consciousness.

For girls with very large breasts, there are only a couple of options. If you are overweight (see Chapter 3), working to reach a normal weight is the first step. If your weight is already normal, then your first step would be to find a bra that minimizes and supports your breasts. Look for one with wide shoulder straps and supportive cups. Make sure you don't have any breast tissue sticking out the sides or underneath the bra. Some department stores and lingerie stores have saleswomen who are trained to take measurements and help you select a properly fitting, supportive bra. A proper fit is important for comfort and for appearance.

The last option, but a necessary one for a few girls, is to have breast reduction surgery. This type of surgery is usually performed by a plastic surgeon. It is big surgery (no pun intended) and the decision to proceed should be very carefully thought out. Look for a plastic surgeon who has experience with breast reduction surgeries *and* teen girls. Realize that this type of surgery will always leave large, noticeable scars. But for the young women who really need it, the scars are well worth the improvement in comfort and confidence.

"Is it weird that one of my boobs is bigger than the other?"

Quickie Answer: Nope.

The Full Scoop: As you go through puberty, one breast almost always takes the lead. The other breast may not ever catch up completely, but usually gets pretty close. Most women have one breast that is larger than the other. The discrepancy should not be so much that your bra cup size would be different for each breast. It's kind of like your feet. One is usually bigger, but you still wear the same size on both feet.

Rarely, a girl will have a large discrepancy or breast size difference that's very noticeable, and she can't find a bra that works for both breasts. The easy answer to fixing that is to buy a bra for the bigger size and use an insert or padding to fill out the other side. Specialty stores for breast cancer survivors often have inserts for bathing suits and bras. The last resort, but again necessary for a few girls, is plastic surgery to enlarge the smaller breast or reduce the larger breast, or some combination that evens things out.

"Should I examine my breasts for lumps?"

The Full Scoop: Being familiar with your changing body is important, but doing monthly breast self-exams, as recommended for adult women, isn't really recommended until you are about nineteen or twenty years old. Why not earlier? Because breast cancer is very rare in teen girls, but benign lumps in the breasts come and go. And some teens just have lumpy but normal breast tissue. If you're looking for lumps every month, you'll probably find one eventually; and it can scare you. For most females, finding a lump in the breast will create a lot of anxiety. For teens, in particular, it also leads to a lot of unnecessary procedures and even surgeries. The bottom line is that breast exams cause more trouble than good in the teen years.

If you're worried about breast cancer (and you shouldn't *worry*, but you should be *aware*), there are much more important things to do during your teen years. Research has actually shown that certain healthy behaviors can reduce your risk of getting breast cancer (and other cancers!) later in life. They include avoiding tobacco, avoiding alcohol, and getting regular exercise. **Your teen years are the perfect time to establish these healthy behaviors, for health and for long-term cancer prevention.** Then, as you become an adult, you can add monthly breast self-exams.

What if you discover a lump anyway? You should definitely check in with your doctor. But if your doctor wants to send you straight to the operating room, you might want to get another opinion. A simple ultrasound is usually the best test for diagnosing the cause of the lump. And in most cases, your doctor can just watch the lump for a few months to see if it changes size. Most lumps in teens will either shrink or stay the same, indicating that they are nothing to worry about.

And finally, although you probably don't need to do breast self-exams yet, make sure your mother and the other adult women you care about in your life are doing their part. Breast self-exams are important for adult women because the earlier a cancerous lump is discovered, the better the chance for a cure. Earlier detection of cancer and higher cure rates happen among women who do monthly BSEs and get yearly mammograms (beginning around age forty). So instead of concentrating on *your* breasts for now, remind the adult women you care about to do their breast exam each month and get their mammogram yearly. When it comes to health, you may have a bigger influence on them than their own doctor!

"My nipples are dimpled in most of the time. Is that normal?'

Quickie Answer: It can be.

The Full Scoop: Nipples, like other parts of our body, can be all different shapes and sizes. They can even point in different directions. Like your belly button, you can have innies or outies. Innies are actually called inverted nipples. Although most nipples are outies, innies are just another type of "normal." Even inverted nipples will come out when you are cold. They may also come out with excitement (sexual or otherwise), anxiety, or when they are rubbed or pulled. Sometimes they pop out just because. Have you noticed that your nipples can seem to have a mind of their own sometimes?

There are only a couple of concerns with inverted nipples. First, they can occasionally have some minor irritation from being in a pocket-like environment where they don't get a lot of fresh air. This may cause a mild skin infection that is easily treated with attention to cleansing and sometimes requires an antibiotic ointment. Second, women with inverted nipples sometimes have more difficulty with breast-feeding. But no worries! If you have inverted nipples, your doctor or nurse can offer some things to make breast-feeding easier when that time comes.

"Why do my boobs hurt when I have my period?"

Quickie Answer: **Estrogen.**

The Full Scoop: It's all about hormones. A hormone called estrogen is what makes our breasts grow in the first place. It's also the reason for the tenderness you sometimes feel in your breasts. Remember how sore they were when they first started growing? That was estrogen starting to circulate in your body as you entered puberty. After you start your period, your estrogen levels will change with your menstrual cycle. There is more estrogen circulating in your body and hanging out in your breasts around the time of ovulation and again with the start of a new period. Those are the two times in your cycle when your breasts are most likely to be sensitive. They may also feel a little heavier during that time because they may even have some swelling in the hormonally sensitive tissues.

If the sensitivity is really bothering you, there are a few things you can do to help. First, you can wear a very supportive bra that keeps your breasts from jiggling. A sports bra is good for that. Second, you should decrease or eliminate any caffeine in your diet (in food and drinks). Some people say vitamin E helps, and others just use an over-the-counter pain medication like ibuprofen or acetaminophen. Make sure you check with a parent before you take any medications, though.

Think It Through

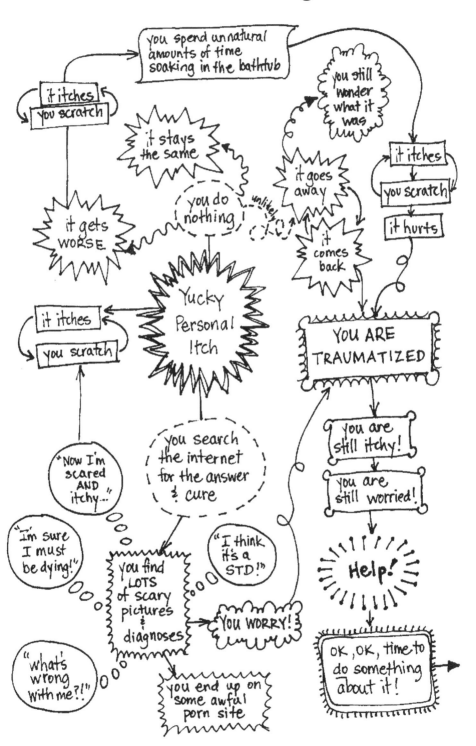

Think It Through

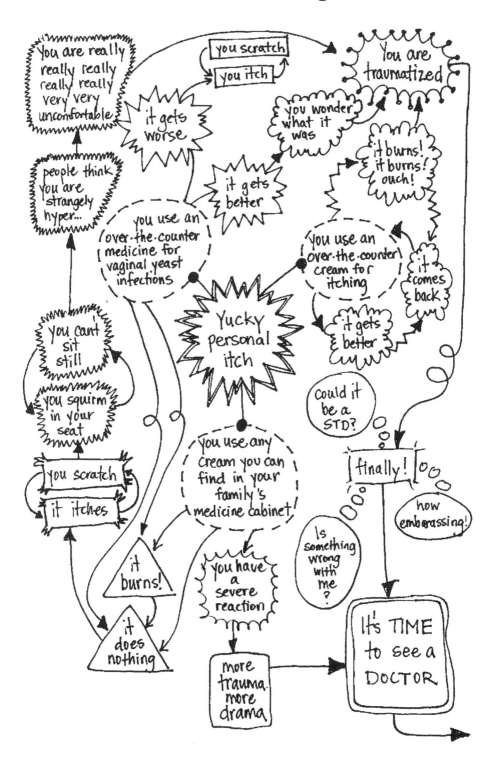

Think It Through

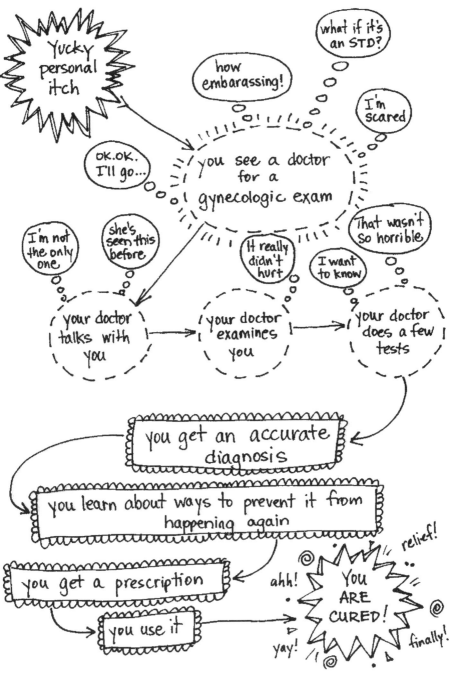

Chapter

3

"Am I normal?"

Body hang-ups
and emotional
meltdowns

A Real-Life Dilemma

Alone in her bedroom, Amanda looked at her desk. There were stacks of textbooks, a laptop cued to MySpace, part of an English paper that was due by Thursday—the one for the book she hadn't finished reading—and review problems for Friday's calculus test. She rolled her eyes at the SAT prep book that she hadn't touched in a week. A bathroom scale sat at the foot of her bed. On the bed was a pair of size two jeans she was determined to fit into by Saturday. It was going to be a long, hungry week.

Amanda inched toward the desk but stopped, sinking squarely to the middle of the floor. *Someday,* she thought, *there had to be more to life than perfect grades, fitting in, and fitting into a pair of jeans.* Reaching behind her, she picked up a hand mirror off the dresser. "Great," she murmured, "dark circles and, oh my God, is that a zit?!" She tossed the mirror aside, but quickly snatched it back up. People always commented on the way she looked. She wasn't being vain; in fact, there were days she wished it wasn't the point. It would be one less thing to worry about.

Staring in the mirror, Amanda examined her almond-shaped eyes, a crazy shade of green, and the ebony hair that would never require a flat iron. It was her mother's striking Asian features, morphed with her father's blond-haired, blue-eyed genes. Personally, she thought it was weird. Everyone else used words like exotic, mysterious—even sexy. Sure, it was flattering, but most of the time, it just made her uncomfortable.

Since mastering Dr. Seuss, Amanda had been more tuned in to books than beauty. She was good at school, never achieving anything less than an A on a report card. But lately, the pressure to make those perfect grades, plus extracurricular activities, and keeping up appearances was getting to be a bit too much. That pressure had led Amanda to some fairly desperate measures.

Tucking her knees tight, she rested her chin on top of them. The second drawer of her desk was directly in her line of vision. "No, no, no . . . it's dangerous and stupid. I'm not doing it again." Then, looking between the mountain of schoolwork and the jeans, she thought it might be the only way to survive and succeed by Saturday. Inside the drawer was a tin of mints, the ordinary kind you buy at the convenience store. But inside the tin were a handful of blue and white capsules. Adderall, according to the stamp on each one; they were the fast track to surviving with no sleep, sharper concentration, and skinnier thighs—or so Amanda had learned.

It wasn't really that dangerous, she thought. It was ADD medication; half the kids at school were on it. But if you didn't need it for ADD, those capsules were like having a personal assistant to do all your work *and* burn all your calories. When Amanda was freaking out over midterms a couple of months ago, Gina Riggins gave her the first one.

She was amazed at how easy it was to get Adderall, easier than real drugs like pot or cocaine. She knew kids who'd done that. Certainly, those drugs were riskier.

Picking one out of the tin, Amanda reached for the glass of water on her nightstand. That and a container of yogurt were the only items on the menu today. If she took the pill, she wouldn't feel hungry. Her stomach wouldn't be growling all afternoon, her mother asking if she'd eaten. She wouldn't have to lie. Maybe that was a good way to look at it. She could stay up until 3:00 AM, get all her work done, and finish that horrid book for English. She might not have to use SparkNotes. Then she wouldn't be cheating. It looked as if the benefits of taking the Adderall outweighed the risks.

• • •

"Amanda, Amanda, wake up!!"

It sounded like somebody was calling her name through a tunnel, a cobwebby, dark tunnel—and, damn, if somebody wasn't slapping her face. Her eyes didn't want to open, but the smell of ammonia was like a shot of adrenaline, and she was suddenly wide awake. There was a semicircle of familiar faces looking down at her: Sydney, Chelsea, Miss Mackie, the health sciences teacher, and Mrs. Gregory, the school nurse. Amanda glanced around, trying to bring things into focus. She was on the floor—the cafeteria floor. Gross! She tried to sit up, but her head seemed to outweigh her entire body.

"Slowly, Amanda, try to sit up slowly," instructed Miss Mackie. With the teacher on one side and Sydney on the other, she managed to get herself into a sitting position.

"I'm okay," she mumbled. "What happened?"

"You fainted," Sydney said.

"Fainted? No way!" Amanda said, noticing the crowd that had gathered. Her cheeks began to burn; Amanda didn't enjoy being the center of attention—under any circumstance.

"Okay, then you decided to take a nap on the cafeteria floor, which I think is worse," said Chelsea.

Glancing at the postlunch floor, Amanda fought a wave of nausea.

"Amanda, if you can stand up for me, I have a wheelchair. I'll take you to the nurse's office," said Mrs. Gregory. With some assistance, she helped herself into the chair and was promptly whisked away.

• • •

Twenty minutes later, Amanda was feeling better with her feet propped up, lying on one of Mrs. Gregory's cots, hidden behind a privacy curtain. "Oh, God, tell me Max Davenport wasn't there," she whispered to Sydney, who had stayed with her. "Just tell me I didn't faint in front of Max."

"Don't change the subject," she said, her arms folded tightly in front of her. Sydney was one of very few friends Amanda confided in. She knew about her secret crush on Lakeside's star hockey player, her lack of eating habits, and, worst of all, the Adderall.

"I may not be as brilliant as you, but I know why you fainted. When was the last time you ate, and how many of those pills have you had today?"

"Keep your voice down!" Propping herself up on her elbows, Amanda tried to peer around the edge of the curtain. "Okay, I had one pill yesterday afternoon and one more this morning. Big deal. I got my English paper done and, well, I *was* ready for my calculus test," she grumbled. "Besides, those pills don't make you faint."

"No, but starving yourself will. And as for your calculus test, I guess you'll be taking the makeup next week, since I'm sure they won't be sending you back to class."

"You're making too much out of it, Syd. So I skipped a couple of meals. I only use the pills when things get really crazy. It's not like I'm addicted."

"Not yet, anyway. I told you, I looked Adderall up on the Internet. It's an amphetamine, Amanda—completely addictive, not to mention illegal without a prescription. What I don't understand is why? You're one of the smartest kids in the whole school, not to mention the prettiest. On top of that, you already have a body to die for. How perfect do you need to be? Because I have to tell you, if this is how you get there, perfect is way overrated."

Doc Talk:
The Way **We See It**

There probably has never been, nor will there ever be, as much change in your life as you experience during your teen years. Your body changes, your friends change, things that stress you out become bigger, and everyone's moods seem to be swinging all around you. So how do you know when change is good (as the saying goes) or when it's abnormal or even dangerous? You have to know what's normal.

The things that people consider normal are influenced by the stuff they see and hear every day. For example, let's say you hang out with a group of people who wear garbage bags as clothing. As the only one not wearing a garbage bag, you begin to feel very out of place. To fit in, you run to the local grocery store and buy some garbage bags. You cut out a head hole and armholes, tie a belt around the waist, and voilà! You look like everyone else, and you feel better about yourself. Do you really look great? But everyone's wearing it. It's *normal,* right? Think again.

When you spend a lot of time looking at magazines, TV, and music videos that feature ultrathin girls with perfect skin and expensive clothes, who look like they are having the best time of their lives, you start to believe they are normal. When you and your friends spend a lot of time talking about your imperfections and how you wish you could change things, it alters your view of what's normal. It makes you think that if you only looked a certain way and dressed a certain way then you'd be having more fun, too. Well, guess what? Normal is NOT what you see in advertisements and on TV. Models represent a very small (and skinny) percentage of our population. Ads are airbrushed to remove zits and cellulite. And even the models themselves can't afford some of the clothes you see them in. **So you have to start realizing that normal is really what you see in your English class, at a basketball game, or at the mall. Look around at real people to know what real is all about.**

When you get mixed up about what is normal, lose sight of reality, and forget about your strengths, you inevitably start to feel bad about yourself. You feel like you're never good enough, and it becomes a chronic struggle. Sometimes, you resort to drastic and even dangerous measures to be thin, "perfect," and to fit in. Focusing on your imperfections and weaknesses can also lead you into things that help you "forget" your hurt and "numb" your pain. That's why girls, in particular, have high rates of depression, drug use, and eating disorders.

There's no easy answer, but you can start to pull away from the negative messages by respecting yourself and appreciating the amazing things your body can do. When you discover what you like about yourself and make that your daily focus, the negative stuff will begin to lose its power over you. Simple things like healthy nutrition, regular exercise, and reducing some of the stress in your life can help. Small steps can make a big difference. Sometimes the first step is the toughest, and it might even require some professional help, but it's definitely possible. When you feel better about yourself, it shows in the way you act and look. And that change IS good.

This chapter will present some body hang-ups and emotional stuff that may bug you. It's all about weight issues, body image, depression and even stretch marks. We hope you don't have any hang-ups, but maybe you have some lingering questions that make you wonder if you're "normal" or not. If your questions aren't answered here, send them to us through our website (www.girlology.com) and we'll try to get the answers posted soon.

YOU
Asked!

"I am so tired of dealing with my acne; will it ever end?"

Quickie Answer: It will get better, we promise!

The Full Scoop: Acne sucks. It's one of those things that happens with puberty but eventually improves over time. Meanwhile, good skin care can reduce the severity. The good news is that eating chocolate and French fries doesn't really make your acne worse. Most of it has to do with genes (did your mom or dad have acne?) and hormones. Here are some tips that may help:

* Wash your face twice a day with a mild soap and water. Don't scrub or use abrasive cleaners: this can make it worse by irritating the skin.

* If you use cover-up look for labels that say the product (makeup, washes, lotions, etc.) is non-acne-forming or noncomedogenic.

* Hair products, especially conditioners and gels, may contain oils that can worsen acne by clogging pores. Make sure you wash your face with soap after you have rinsed your conditioner out. Try to keep gels and other hair products off your face. Your back may be affected by your hair conditioner, so make sure you wash your back well after rinsing the conditioner out of your hair.

* Watch out for things that touch or rub your face. Helmet straps, telephones, hands, and hats can clog and irritate your pores and make acne worse.

* Do not pick, pinch, or pop zits. It can cause scarring.

* Do what you can to decrease the stress in your life. Yep, stress can worsen acne by increasing oil production.

* Periods can definitely affect your acne. It's hormonal. Know when your period is due and take extra time with your skin care.

* Try an over-the-counter product containing benzoyl peroxide, salicylic acid, or tea tree oil. They may cause dry or flaking skin, but they can be very helpful for some. If you need moisturizer on your face because of the flaking, make sure it is noncomedogenic or non-acne-forming. (Check the label.)

Sometimes, no matter how hard you try, your acne just does not go away. As we said, some girls need more than just washing and cleansers because of genetics. If you are taking care of your skin and acne is still a big problem for you, get help. Doctors have great medicines that work, but realize that they may take four to six weeks before you see an improvement. Don't give up or expect a miracle in a few days.

"I have hair on my chin and mustache area. It's so embarrassing. What can I do?"

Quickie Answer: There are several safe ways to remove the hair, but you need to be certain that the hair growth is not related to a medical problem.

The Full Scoop: Genetics determine how hairy you are. Is your dad hairy? Do your parents have an ethnic background where people typically have dark hair or a dark complexion? Those are the most common reasons for facial hair, and there's nothing wrong with you if that's your reason. But there are some medical conditions that can cause excessive hair growth in girls and women.

The most common medical condition that causes this is called polycystic ovarian syndrome (PCOS). With PCOS, the hair growth usually shows up around puberty and may involve the face, chest, back, arms, abdomen, and upper legs. If you find that you have excess hair, worsening acne, and you skip months without your period, you may want to talk to your doctor about the possibility of having PCOS.

Removing hair from the face and chin can be more difficult than from your legs or armpits. You probably won't want to shave your face because you'd have to do it every day, sometimes twice a day. And razor stubble can be embarrassing. There are plenty of other methods to try:

* Plucking works well; it's free, and you can do it yourself. You don't get the same stubble as shaving because you pull the hairs out by the roots.
* Bleach creams will lighten the hair and make it less noticeable.
* Cream depilatories will remove the hair but can cause skin irritation.
* Waxing will remove the hair from its roots so the results last longer. You can do this at home or get it done at a salon. It's a little painful, but it's fast and effective.
* Electrolysis or laser hair removal will permanently reduce the amount of hair, but these methods are expensive and can be painful.
* You can get a prescription cream that stops the hair growth at the

root. You have to use it twice a day, every day, or the hair grows back. It's also fairly expensive.

✳ For girls with PCOS, birth control pills will also help reduce new facial hair growth but won't do anything to get rid of the hair that is already there.

✳ You can get a prescription pill (spironolactone) that decreases hair growth. It takes about three months to notice the difference, and you need to stay on it as long as you want the results.

Whatever the reason, many girls are very bothered by facial hair. Getting rid of it can boost your confidence.

"My doctor says I'm at a good weight, but why do I still feel fat?"

Quickie Answer: It's hard to get real about what's normal.

The Full Scoop: First of all, you're not the only one who feels like that. Among girls who are a normal weight, 50 to 70 percent of them believe they are overweight. The media may have a lot to do with that.

Images of girls' bodies are everywhere. Women and their body parts sell everything from cars to food to men's underwear to beauty products. What's up with that? The marketing industry has learned that making girls and women feel insecure about themselves makes them buy stuff that will supposedly make them feel better. They want to make you believe that if you use their product or wear their clothes, you'll be happier. Their goal is to get you to spend your money on the products they are selling. But normal people don't usually look the same in their clothes and with their products, so it's really an unattainable beauty they're promoting. **If they keep showing you the unattainable, you'll never be satisfied, and you'll keep on buying stuff—get it?** Doesn't it make you mad?

The average model is 5 feet 11 inches and weighs about 110 pounds. The average woman is 5 feet 4 inches and weighs 145 pounds. That is a big difference. Only 2 percent of our population looks like the models on TV and in magazines. Oh, and don't forget they also use airbrushing and lighting to perfect their look. Ever wonder why they don't ever have stretch marks or zits? They have the power of airbrushing and computer enhancement to fix it all, which is unattainable in real life.

So many girls feel fat because they can never reach the ultrathin appearance of all the images they see. For a reality check, just look around your school cafeteria. That's what normal is all about. Start noticing what you LIKE about your body, not what you don't like. The more you focus on your good parts, the better you will feel about yourself. When you feel good about yourself, others notice, too! **And while you're at it, start noticing the good stuff about your friends, too.** Start a beauty revolution—and keep it real.

"How can I tell what is a healthy weight for me?"

Quickie Answer: Your body mass index (BMI) is more important than your weight.

The Full Scoop: Your weight doesn't mean a whole lot without considering your height. BMI uses both height and weight, and it's the best measurement to determine whether you are overweight, underweight, or obese (very overweight). For teens, a normal BMI changes with your age because your body changes so much as you go through your teen years.

To calculate your BMI, you need to know your accurate height and weight. The original formula used kilograms and meters, but here's the formula that lets you use pounds and inches:

$$\text{BMI} = \text{weight (pounds)} / \text{height (inches)}^2 \times 703$$

If that's too much math, you can go to www.cdc.gov and enter "teen BMI calculator" in the search box. You'll get a list of possible pages. Go to the one that says "BMI for Children and Teens" and calculate your own using the calculator on that page.

Once you know your BMI, you'll need to plot it on the chart on the next page to see your percentile for your age. If your BMI is at the 50th percentile, then you are average for your age-group. If your BMI is less than the 5th percentile or greater than the 85th percentile, you should see your doctor for recommendations.

BMI is a good resource for teens who may feel overweight, but it does have its limitations. Your BMI may be higher if you are very muscular or if you have a large frame. On the other hand, if you are a smaller person with a small frame, your BMI could be normal even though you may have too much body fat. These are good reasons to discuss your BMI with your doctor.

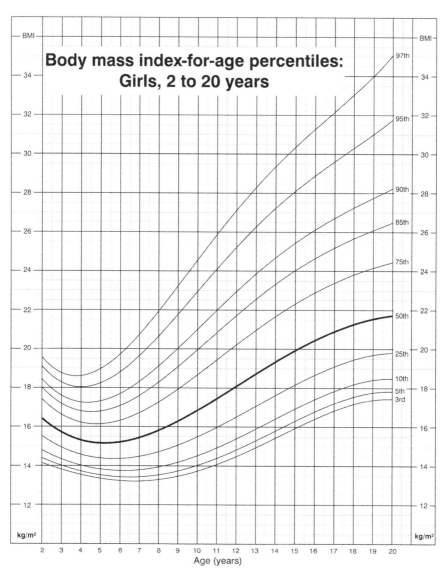

Body mass index-for-age percentiles: Girls, 2 to 20 years

Published May 30, 2000.
SOURCE: Developed by the National Center for Health Statistics in collaboration with the National Center for Chronic Disease Prevention and Health Promotion (2000).

"What is a safe diet pill?"

Quickie Answer: **There are no "safe" diet pills.**

The Full Scoop: About one in four girls will use diet pills at some point to help them lose weight. We hate to break it to you, but **diet pills aren't a quick and easy fix to your weight problems.** The pills may help you eat less and lose weight at first, but once your body gets used to them, they stop working. Guess what happens next? You gain back all the weight, and most girls gain even more because they haven't changed their eating habits. Not only are diet pills ineffective in losing weight, they can kill you! Many of the current diet pills out there can cause these dangerous side effects: high blood pressure, dizziness, headaches, not sleeping well (insomnia), depression, anxiety, blurred vision, heart palpitations, and irregular heartbeats.

Fat blockers are another form of diet pills. Taking them will usually cause gas, bloating, and diarrhea—sometimes even uncontrollable diarrhea. How gross would that be? These may also cause vitamin deficiencies because they block certain fats that help us absorb vitamins from our food. Without these vitamins, you could have dry skin and hair loss. They're just not worth it.

The so-called "natural" and herbal diet pills are also dangerous, especially for teen girls. Even some of the diet pill labels warn teens not to take them. Most of these have high doses of caffeine in them. None of these pills are regulated or tested by the government for safety. The Food and Drug Administration (FDA) banned the popular appetite suppressant ephedra after it was linked to the deaths of 155 people. Now ephedra has been replaced by other untested ingredients that could be just as dangerous.

"How do I know if I really have an eating disorder?"

The Full Scoop: There are two major groups of eating disorders: anorexia and bulimia. Some girls have elements of both. **Anorexia is characterized by a significant weight loss from excessive dieting and restricting calories.** Girls with anorexia feel fat no matter how thin they may be. They are very preoccupied with food and their weight, but they find ways to ignore their feelings of hunger. The scariest thing is that 10 to 20 percent of girls with this disease will eventually die from complications related to starving themselves.

Anorexia can start off as an innocent attempt to lose a little weight. The attention and compliments that come with the weight loss feel good. So then they start to believe that losing more would make them even happier. But no matter how much weight is lost, it is never enough. They never seem to be happy or satisfied. Sometimes by focusing so much on weight loss and food, they can ignore bigger problems that are too painful to deal with. The weight loss becomes excessive and a controlling force in their lives.

Bulimia is characterized by a cycle of binge eating followed by purging to try to rid the body of the unwanted calories. A binge may be different for each person. One person's binge may be three cheeseburgers, supersize fries, and a half gallon of ice cream. Another's may be one cookie. A purge may be different for each person as well. Purging can be attempted through vomiting, laxative abuse, excessive exercise, fasting, or using diuretics, diet pills, and enemas.

With bulimia, food becomes a source of comfort. Hoarding and bingeing on food may become a way of blocking or letting out feelings. The binge brings on terrible guilt, so bulimics purge to rid themselves of all the calories. Usually they vow to never binge again, but the cycle begins again when they feel out of control. Sometimes it takes years to break the cycle completely.

Below is a list of signs and symptoms of eating disorders. This list may help you recognize an eating disorder in yourself or someone else.

* Losing weight quickly or having a weight that fluctuates
* Talking about being fat ALL THE TIME
* Spending a lot of time reading food labels, memorizing calorie contents, and studying recipes
* Feeling like you have to be perfect at everything
* Eating very little, secretly eating, or making excuses for not eating
* Spending a lot of time in the bathroom
* Exercising excessively
* Using alcohol, diet pills, or illegal drugs to lose weight
* Avoiding social events that involve food
* Weighing yourself frequently and allowing your weight to affect your moods
* Having symptoms of depression, irritability, or even mood swings

There are also medical complications that are associated with eating disorders. These are:

* Lack of energy
* Irregular period or no period at all
* Headaches
* Constipation and diarrhea
* Hair loss

* Dizziness
* Sores on the knuckles from inducing vomiting
* Appearance of fine downy hair on back and face
* Stomach pain
* Tooth decay and loss of enamel from frequent vomiting
* Life-threatening things such as kidney and liver damage, anemia, low blood pressure, loss of bone mass, and possibly cardiac arrest and death

As you can see, this is a very scary and serious illness. If you know anyone who has these signs or symptoms, or you have these yourself, the first step to getting better is to tell someone. Anorexia and bulimia are diseases that can be treated with proper therapy and medical attention, but the treatment is very difficult for many girls with anorexia to accept. Relapses are common, and the treatment may take several years. A dedicated and experienced therapist is important. With therapy and medical attention, most of the complications are reversed, resulting in proper weight gain and changes in eating habits.

"My doctor says my stretch marks will disappear, but they haven't. What can I do?"

The Full Scoop: **Unfortunately, not much.** Stretch marks are a normal part of growth and usually show up when your body grows rapidly during puberty or with a drastic change in your body weight.

Skin is usually elastic (meaning stretchy), but too much stretch on the tissues underneath the skin can cause stretch marks. They usually start as a streak or line that looks red to dark pink to purple. With time, the color fades and eventually they become lighter and less noticeable.

Most teen girls and adult women have stretch marks somewhere on their bodies. There are a few girls out there who will never get any. Lucky genetics. The most common places you'll see them are on your breasts, buttocks, hips, and thighs. Some women don't get any stretch marks until pregnancy, when their belly grows quickly. Even guys can get them. Medications containing steroids can also cause or worsen them.

The good news is that stretch marks will fade and sometimes disappear over time. If you are just noticing some, you may need to change your clothing style for a little while to keep them covered up. Keeping them covered is also a good idea because exposing them to sunlight or light from a tanning bed can make them look worse. Stretch marks won't tan, so they might become more noticeable if the rest of your skin is tanned or darker. Some girls find that sunless tanning lotions and sprays can help camouflage them.

Myth Bust!

There are creams that make stretch marks disappear.

FALSE! FALSE! FALSE!

Don't waste your money. All stretch marks will fade over time, so just try to be patient. The only way to really get rid of them is through plastic surgery techniques, which can be expensive and painful, and are not recommended for teens anyway.

"I sweat too much. Is one deodorant better than others?"

Quickie Answer: You don't need just a deodorant; you need more antiperspirant.

The Full Scoop: Sweating a lot during your teen years is pretty common, but just knowing that doesn't help you, does it? As a teen, your sweat glands and oil-producing glands work overtime and all the time. The sweat glands make you wet, while the oil-producing glands provide the smells because of the breakdown of the oils by natural bacteria on the skin. Nice.

So how do you handle all this wetness and odor? Well, start with a daily bath or shower and use soap in all those areas. We assume you've already done that much. So, next you need a good deodorant/antiperspirant. The deodorant part keeps the smell away and the antiperspirant helps with all the wetness.

Antiperspirants work by blocking or plugging up your sweat glands. It's okay and even recommended that you apply it to dry underarms in the morning and at night if necessary. If you're only going to use it once a day, applying it at night is more effective than just in the morning.

Wearing clothes made of natural fibers can help, too. Cotton keeps you cool but absorbs water easily and may stay wet for a longer time. Synthetic fibers may be warmer with less breathing, but they help draw sweat away from the body to make you look drier. It also helps to keep an extra shirt around for those really bad days.

If that still doesn't do the trick, there are prescription-strength antiperspirants available through your doctor. Make sure you follow your doctor's advice if using these.

"I'm sixteen and most girls in my class are taller than me. Will I grow any taller?"

Quickie Answer: Maybe not. Adult height is determined by many factors. These include genetics (how tall are your parents, grandparents, and siblings?) and your overall health and nutrition.

The Full Scoop: The average height for adult women is about 5 feet 4 inches, but there is a huge range of what's normal. Most girls grow about two to two-and-a-half inches per year from age two until puberty. At puberty, there is a growth spurt. Most girls start growing more rapidly around eleven, and then slow down by age thirteen or so. Some girls, however, will continue growing until they are sixteen to eighteen years old. The interesting thing about growth is that you grow pretty rapidly from the start of puberty up until about six months before you start your period. Once you start your period, your growth slows down a lot but doesn't necessarily stop for a few more years. Having a yearly checkup by your doctor can help you understand your own growth pattern as well as help predict your adult height.

"Why do I get tiny red bumps on my legs when I shave?"

Quickie Answer: Razor burn, nicks, cuts, and ingrown hairs are all side effects of shaving.

The Full Scoop: Deciding to remove body hair is a personal choice, and shaving is the most common method for removing leg, underarm, and groin hair. The results only last for one to three days because shaving just removes the tip of the hair that has grown above the skin surface. Sometimes during shaving the hair can get pushed back into the follicle, the skin itself can get scraped, or the follicle can get irritated. These problems are what cause that annoying razor rash and may cause ingrown hairs. Follow our suggestions on page 55 to help avoid these problems.

"My friend acts all sad and needy. How can I tell if she wants attention or if she's really depressed?"

Quickie Answer: Don't try to be a therapist; she may need professional help.

The Full Scoop: The teen years are full of emotional ups and downs. Feelings of sadness, hopelessness, and despair are common, but if they interfere with normal activities, it could be true depression. About one in four girls will show symptoms of **depression, and it's twice as common among girls than boys.** So it's very likely that you will encounter a friend who is depressed at some point during your teen years. It can help to know the warning signs, which are:

* Feeling sad, being tearful, and crying most of the time
* Feeling like life is not worth living

* Feeling worthless, hopeless, or useless

* Losing interest in things that used to be fun

* Having a low energy level, boredom, and feeling tired all the time

* Losing connections with friends and family or feeling like relationships are not important

* Feeling major guilt over small things

* Acting irritable, angry, or hostile

* Not caring about anything in the present or future

* Having trouble concentrating

* Experiencing changes in eating or sleeping patterns

* Using alcohol or other drugs to try to feel better

* Physical problems such as stomachaches, headaches, loss of appetite, weight gain, or loss

* Self-destructive behavior (cutting, unprotected sex, unsafe driving)

* Thoughts of suicide

Most teens will show at least a couple of these symptoms at some point. When there is true depression, there will be many of these symptoms going on daily for at least a few weeks. Treatment for depression is very important, especially if there are signs of self-destructive behavior or suicidal thoughts. **Be your friend's advocate, because there may be no one else.** Talk with a trusted adult, such as a school counselor, a coach, a teacher, a youth leader, or a parent. It is important to realize that depression is common and has severe consequences if not treated.

Treatment can include talk therapy, medication, or both. It is up to a professional to decide what is best for each person. If talk therapy is recommended, it doesn't mean the depressed person is "crazy." Just as things can go wrong with other parts of the body, things can go a little haywire in the brain. Treatment can change that. Get help!

"How does cutting make someone feel better?"

Quickie Answer: **This is serious. Read on.**

The Full Scoop: Currently in America, about 10 percent of teen girls are cutting. It's serious, because girls who cut themselves usually have other dangerous behaviors and are often dealing with some heavy emotional problems. They say they do it because they don't know any other way to cope with strong emotions like depression, anger, shame, and frustration. These emotions may result from bad relationships, abuse, or intense peer pressure. Some don't even know why they have these negative emotions.

For cutters, they usually don't know how to deal with their emotions, so they hurt themselves to find relief or comfort. That doesn't seem to make sense does it? There can be different reasons for it: bad coping abilities, a way to "wake up" from a numbing emotional experience, or simply an attempt to relieve the pain of a bad experience or to hurt themselves as punishment. For some, though, it's just a way to seem rebellious and radical.

Whatever the reason, **cutting only provides a temporary solution. It's not normal, and it's not cool.** Cutting is a cry for help, but once it's discovered, it can be a wake-up call for some. Most girls admit that the first step is the hardest—telling someone. A trusted adult should be able to help you find a professional. That's what it will take to begin the healing process. Treatment can help you understand the triggers that start the cutting in the first place, but realize that it will take some work on your part. Getting treatment or help is important.

"I'm pretty sure I have ADD. Can I ask my doctor for a prescription?"

Quickie Answer: You'll need an evaluation first, but your doctor is a good place to start.

The Full Scoop: The most common characteristics of attention deficit/hyperactive disorder (ADHD) or ADD in teen girls are school struggles, difficulty focusing or staying on track, impulsive behaviors, disorganization, and forgetting or "not hearing" assignments or instructions. Does this sound like you? Sound like your friends? Maybe. But actually, only 5 percent of all people really have ADD or ADHD.

Sometimes other things going on in your life can cause you to have some of the ADHD or ADD symptoms. Depression and anxiety are two of the most common. School problems could also be related to a learning disorder, drugs, or substance use. Other medical problems should also be considered. That's why it's important to have a doctor involved in the evaluation.

If you really do have ADD or ADHD, treatment is important and usually involves a combination of talking therapy and medications. The medication that seems most effective is in a category of medicines called stimulants. If taken in the proper dose, the stimulants won't make you feel high, just more focused. The most common side effects include sleep problems, headache, decreased appetite, anxiety, mood swings, or stomachaches. Obviously, if you need these meds, they can be helpful, but if you don't, they can be dangerous.

"If I keep looking at the girls dressing in the locker room, do you think that means I'm gay?"

Quickie Answer: Nope. It takes more than that.

The Full Scoop: As a teen, it's probably just curiosity when you look at other girls as they are dressing or undressing. It's normal to want to know if your body looks like other girls, so looking is one way you reassure yourself that your body is normal. On the other hand, if you are looking at nude girls and you feel sexually excited by it, it might have a different meaning. Even if a girl experiments sexually with another girl, it doesn't necessarily mean she is gay. **Sexuality is more complicated than that.** You really have to consider whether you are attracted in a romantic way to men, women, or both. That's what really determines your sexual orientation, and that can take time. Most research shows that gay or lesbian adults noticed their attraction to the same sex during their teen years. Interestingly, a lot of teens are not sure whether they are gay or not, but by the time they are adults, most are certain of their sexual orientation. The confusion can be tough to handle during your teen years, so it's important to find an adult you trust to confide in.

We're not here to argue whether being gay is a choice you make or you're just born that way. We know it's never an easy life because of prejudice and intolerance in our society. What's most important to realize is that sexual orientation is just a part of who a person really is. Just because someone is gay doesn't change their value as an individual or their contributions to our society. Remember what we said in our first book, "*Love is love.* We can't always help who we fall in love with. The world is filled with enough hatred and violence. We should never hate people for loving others, even if it means they are gay."

Think It Through

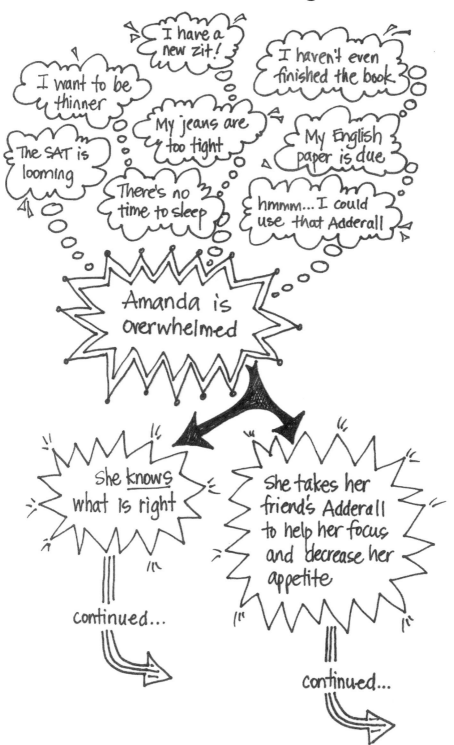

Think It Through

to review...

Amanda is overwhelmed

She takes her friend's Adderall

she misses a test

she faints

her grades drop

She can skip meals & not feel hungry

what a MESS

she has energy

she gets her work done

she thinks it is helping

she feels BAD about herself

She takes MORE Adderall

she feels addicted

she KNOWS what is right...

she gets depressed

she needs treatment

she finally begins to learn about stress management & develop a healthier body image...

Think It Through

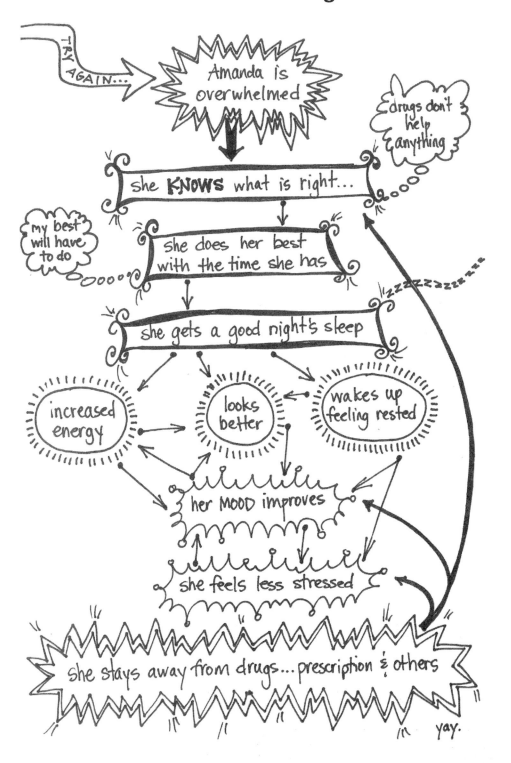

Chapter

"Is sex really such a big deal?"

Reality check

A Real-Life Dilemma

Tasha, Chelsea, and Amanda finally convinced Sydney that Aidan was only using her to service his needs. And Sydney finally realized they were right. When Sydney confronted Aidan and told him she would no longer be accommodating him in any sexual way, she expected it would be over.

A slack-jawed look of amazement and disbelief hung from his gorgeous face. And then, as she expected, he totally dumped her. And really, it was okay. It actually felt good to stand her ground. At first, Sydney had to force herself, remind herself not to think about Aidan 24/7. She found that putting her energy into her friends, schoolwork, and even a community service project helped put Aidan in perspective. She even spent a weekend volunteering for Habitat for Humanity—an activity that was so not Aidan Scofield. Sydney was surrounded by her friends and her mom, who helped her realize there were more important things in life than having a BF. She was able to drive past his street without turning in to go by his house, and she even quit checking her phone for missed text messages. Things were normal again. Sydney had thoroughly embraced the idea that life would go on without Aidan.

Then, one afternoon, he called. They were a good three minutes into the conversation when she realized that he was apologizing. Amazing. He said he wanted a second chance to prove he really cared about her and invited her to dinner at his parents' country club. She turned him down. Sydney really wasn't that into him anymore.

But she soon learned that besides being the senior class hottie, Aidan was also persistent. A ride, he only wanted to give her a ride home from school. When she said okay, his face lit up like she'd offered to sleep with him—like that was ever going to happen! Then, two days later, he stood by her locker practically begging her to go to the movies, swearing he was a changed person. Of course, she didn't believe him, but she was dying to see the new Johnny Depp movie, so she agreed.

To her surprise, Aidan was a perfect gentleman, barely kissing her good night. It was right around then when Sydney started to sway the other way. She did like Aidan—maybe more than she was willing to admit. He made her feel so many things. And the more he behaved, the more Sydney found she wished he wouldn't. On the fourth hand-holding date, she'd had about enough of purity-boy and practically jumped Aidan, planting a huge kiss on him. He blinked, seemingly stunned by the show of affection.

"Well, aren't you going to kiss me back?" she asked.

"Yeah . . . of course." But as he bent forward to her waiting mouth, he stopped. "I don't want to screw this up, Syd. I really like you."

"I get that. But Aidan, I'm starting to wonder if you want to date me or be my big brother."

After a dumbstruck moment, he grinned. "Date you, definitely date you." And finally, he offered the kiss she'd been waiting on for weeks.

• • •

Things heated up after that. A little more than a month into the relationship, Sydney hit a wall—a big, hot, I-want-to-know-what's-on-the-other-side wall. The way Aidan was on her mind began to change. She was no longer content with doodling his name in the margin of her notebook or being known as the girl who'd tamed Aidan Scofield. Sydney found herself wondering what it might be like to have sex with him. She was curious, so curious, as to what all the commotion was about. And it seemed like everyone else was doing it. Well, everyone except Tasha, Amanda, and Chelsea. But one of them had to be first, right?

Then, on a regular Friday, when Sydney thought the highlight was going to be her new watermelon rush nail polish, they did it—they had sex. It was sort of, kind of, planned. They had a condom, Aidan's parents weren't home, and there was nothing on TV. They didn't discuss it much beforehand—and not so much afterward either. It wasn't awful, not like some of the horror stories she'd heard. But it wasn't anything particularly special either. It oddly wasn't what Sydney had been hoping for, especially the after part. Aidan was nice enough. He even thanked her. And Sydney felt a little empty, like she'd given away something huge to satisfy a momentary itch—hers and his.

• • •

A few days later, on a regular Monday, the four girls were hanging out in Tasha's bedroom. They had just finished discussing Dawn

Antinelli's secret tattoo when Sydney blurted it out: "I did it. I had sex with Aidan." But her eyes never veered off Tasha's CD collection; it wasn't like she was looking for their approval. It got quieter than Sydney would have liked, and she could feel their collective stare. She knew Tasha would be first with an opinion.

"You did what? Are you out of your mind?"

"You heard me," she said with a gulp. "We did it. And . . . well, I . . ."

"You what?" Amanda said, her eyes popping wider than Sydney had ever seen. "Don't tell me you didn't use anything?"

"No, it's not . . . I'm not worried about that." She bit her lower lip, her brow furrowing at them. "Well, not too much anyway. We used a condom, I'm sure it's fine . . . But I guess you really can't be 100 percent sure until you get your period. But what, condoms are like 99 percent effective, right?"

"Uh, more like 85 percent, Syd," said Tasha, who always seemed to have up-to-the-minute stats.

"Damn, Syd, I know he's really hot and he really likes you. But I can't believe you'd let him convince you to . . ."

"It wasn't all Aidan's idea. It was sorta mine."

"Yours?" Chelsea said, scooting a little closer to Sydney. "So, what was it like? Did it, um, hurt?" she asked in a tiny voice.

"No . . . yes, maybe a little. And, honestly, it was over quicker than you might expect. But that part didn't bother me so much. I have to tell you, the buildup is a lot more intense than the bang . . . if you know what I mean." Looking at their blank expressions, Sydney could tell they didn't have a clue what she meant. "It was okay. But you know, it wasn't like the Rock'n'Roller Coaster at Disney or anything."

Amanda shook her head. "You lost me, Syd. What does that have to do with . . ."

"Well, you know how you'd get right back in line to go again, because it was so great?" They got that, collectively nodding. "I'm not so sure I would. At least not with Aidan."

"And why's that?" Tasha asked, her arms folding in a way that just kind of said, *I told you so.*

But it was Chelsea who jumped in with an answer. "Because she did it out of curiosity and pheromones—they make you horny."

"I did it why?" Sydney asked, wondering if Chelsea really had the answer to a question she'd been asking herself for days, or if she'd just read one too many articles in *Cosmo.*

"It's simple: you like Aidan; he likes you. We get that. I mean, who wouldn't want to do it with Aidan Scofield?" As Tasha's hand shot up, they all giggled. "He's great looking, popular, and he's gone out of his way to redeem himself. I'll give him that. But how do you feel about him, Syd? I mean, other than the bonus points I just rattled off."

"Or was it just more about curiosity and Aidan being a great candidate?" asked Tasha.

"Well," she said hesitantly. "I do like Aidan. But I think, more than that, I was just curious. I just wanted to know what it was all about."

"And now?" said Chelsea.

"And now I wish I had thought it through more. It's funny; the actual sex part wasn't that big a deal. But how I feel now, I didn't think I'd feel like this. And I don't know that it's going to change anytime soon."

Doc Talk:
The Way **We See It**

THE MESSAGES YOU HEAR ABOUT SEX are so mixed up that it's hard to know whether sex is really a big deal or no big deal. Everyone has an opinion. Your parents probably say it's a big deal, don't do it. You friends may say it's no big deal, go for it. And on TV, the Internet, and chat rooms, everyone's doing it, done it, or talking about it. No wonder Sydney was curious. How can one little three-letter word generate such controversy and confusion?

Whether you want it to be or not, sex is a big deal because it can have lifelong consequences. The possibility of something great like creating a new life—or of something horrible like getting an infection—make it nearly impossible to experience sex as something purely physical with no "emotional" strings attached. Especially as a girl, that potential for creating a life connects sex with your emotions on a level that is so deep and instinctual that you don't have much control over it. If you're living in the moment without thinking about the future, it's easy to get trapped. *Wanna have sex? Hook up? Have fun? Feel good?* Maybe. But **in the midst of all the physical excitement and pleasure, there's the possibility of so many things going wrong:** pregnancy in a relationship that isn't ready to provide for a baby, infections that can be painful and embarrassing, feeling like you need affection and love that's not really there for you.

It's normal to be curious about sex or even think you are ready for it. It's what led Sydney to try it. But if you are not in a mature relationship where there is emotional connection, commitment, and protection against unwanted consequences, then having sex out of curiosity, or for the sheer physical pleasure of it, will disappoint you and leave you feeling empty.

We hope this chapter will help answer some of the questions you may have about sex and sexual stuff. Maybe some of your curiosity will be satisfied by some of our answers. And if you have more questions, send them our way through our website at www.girlology.com. We hope that it all helps you recognize that sex really is a big deal, and it's worth waiting for the right time.

YOU Asked!

"Am I the only girl who isn't having sex?"

Quickie Answer: No, not as many teens have sex as you might think.

The Full Scoop: If you haven't had sex, it may sometimes feel like you are the only teen around who hasn't. We can reassure you that you're not alone. Among all girls in high school, less than half have ever had sex. So you're actually in the majority. By the time you graduate, though, more than half in your senior class will have had sex, but there's still a large number who choose to wait. And we would also like to congratulate you on your decision. Obviously the number of kids who choose to have sex increases with each increasing grade, so the pressure seems to increase, too.

"Does sex hurt the first time?"

Quickie Answer: **It depends.**

The Full Scoop: Sex can be painful for some girls and women for lots of different reasons. As you can imagine, your vagina doesn't just automatically accept an erect penis. So if your body isn't totally prepared and ready for sex, it can hurt. How do you get "prepared"? **For girls, most of the preparation has to happen in the brain before it happens in the vaginal area.** For the vagina to become relaxed and lubricated enough, the brain has to send the signals that say, "I am feeling safe. I'm liking this activity. I'm not worried about anything. I feel good about what I'm doing. Yes. Yes. Yes. This is all good." But if there are any signals in there that say, "This is feeling good, but I'm not so sure. I'm scared. I'm embarrassed. I'm going to get into so much trouble if my parents find out. I might never see this guy again and then what will I do if I'm pregnant? Is the condom on right? What am I doing? I'm not supposed to be doing this . . ." Get the picture? Anyway, if the brain is sending those negative signals, the vagina can tighten up a little and the lubrication can even slow down or stop. That makes sex more physically painful, and there's obviously some emotional angst going on as well.

Even if you get through the preparation and everything is "go" in your brain, sex can still be uncomfortable at first. It takes time and experience in a healthy relationship before most girls actually start enjoying sex.

"Do you always bleed after having sex for the first time?"

Quickie Answer: Not always, but it is common.

The Full Scoop: Even for females who may be completely prepared for sex (see above), there is usually some bleeding after the first time. That's because the hymen will often need to tear a little to allow an erect penis into the vaginal opening. For some women who have never had sex, there may not be any bleeding because the hymen was able to stretch enough without tearing, or it may have been torn previously during other activities, particularly mutual masturbation. **Other than after the first time, bleeding after sex is NOT normal.** When there's bleeding after sex any other time, it could signal a sexually transmitted disease, pregnancy, cancer or precancer, an injury, or something wrong in the uterus. It's important to see your doctor to figure out why.

"What exactly is an erection?"

Quickie Answer: The medical term for a boner, a hard-on, or a woody.

The Full Scoop: When a guy is sexually aroused, there is increased blood flow to the penis and it becomes stiff and erect. A penis has three parts: the urethra where urine comes out and two cylinder-shaped parts called the erectile bodies. When a guy is sexually excited, his blood flows into the erectile bodies and makes the penis become harder, longer, and wider. And no, there are no bones involved.

An erection can seem like an odd thing at times. You may notice your BF or other guys putting their hand in their pocket or trying to rearrange themselves. Erections can occur anytime, but especially when you are kissing, hugging, or even when he is just thinking about sex (which happens a lot!). Anything that sexually arouses a guy may cause an erection, and sometimes they just happen randomly.

Erections can go away on their own, or they end with ejaculation. Ejaculation (also known as "coming" or climaxing) is when a guy expels semen from his penis during an orgasm. The semen squirts out of the urethra (which is his pee hole, right?). So, can a guy urinate at the same time that he is ejaculating? Nope. As ejaculation starts, a small valve closes off the bladder. He can't ejaculate and urinate at the same time.

"If a guy has an erection, does he have to come?"

Quickie Answer: NO, and don't let him tell you he does.

The Full Scoop: As we said above, sometimes guys have erections without any sexual thoughts or feelings at all. These go away quickly if the guy can think of something to get his mind off of his erection. If it is during a sexual thought or act, he can still take care of it himself, either by thinking about something not sexual, mas-turbating, or taking a cold shower! Guys may say they have to come if the erection has lasted a long time or if you two have been making out heavily for a while, **but remember: it is never YOUR responsibility to make sure he ejaculates.**

"What exactly is 'come'"?

Quickie Answer: **Semen.**

The Full Scoop: Ejaculation releases "come" or semen (which is a bet-ter word for it). Semen has about 200 to 500 million sperm in each ejaculation. Remember, it only takes one sperm to make a baby. The sperm makes up a small portion (about 5 percent) of the total flu-ids that are released (it's about a teaspoon). The rest of the fluid has other stuff in it like metal and salt ions, sugar, lipids, steroid hormones, enzymes, prostaglandin hormones, and amino acids. Is that too much information?

Semen is also the way many STDs are spread, because it's where viruses (like HIV) and bacteria (like chlamydia) live. So, it is not just skin-to-skin contact that causes certain STDs. You have to stay away from the semen. You can read more about STDs in Chapter 8.

"So, what is 'pre-come'"?

The Full Scoop: This is another word for pre-ejaculate. It is a clear fluid that is released from a guy's penis when he is sexually excited. It occurs during masturbation, foreplay, or in the early stages of sex. Pre-ejaculation obviously happens before a guy has an orgasm and releases his semen. This fluid may carry infections and some sperm in it, so you still need to treat it the same as semen, and that means avoiding contact with it by using a condom to contain it, or just stay away from it.

"My BF says he has to come at least twice a week or he gets 'blue balls.'"

Quickie Answer: Are you kidding? Not so!

The Full Scoop: Guys call it "blue balls" if they have been sexually aroused but haven't ejaculated. It gives them a heavy sensation or uncomfortable ache in their testicles (which is a better term for balls). It is a real condition, but their testicles definitely do not turn blue. In fact, the sensation disappears in time. Blue balls don't happen with every erection, although a guy may tell you differently. Make sure you never let a guy talk you into sexual stuff to relieve his blue balls. He knows how to take care of that all by himself.

"What's so wrong about having sex when you're younger?"

The Full Scoop: There are lots of reasons, both physical and emotional, why it's important to avoid sex until you are an adult. When you are a teen, your body is physically more at risk for problems related to pregnancy and STDs. If you get pregnant as a teen (and one in three girls who have sex as a teen will get pregnant by age twenty), you are at risk for more complications (like premature babies, infant death, and toxemia) than adult women experience.

As a teen, you are also more at risk for getting sexually transmitted infections than an adult exposed to the same thing. Why? The cells on the cervix (which is at the end of your vagina and is the opening to your uterus) are still in the process of maturing and growing. Their immaturity and location leaves them more exposed and susceptible to certain infections. Sexually transmitted infections are the most common cause of health problems among adolescent girls, as well as infertility (meaning you can't get pregnant) and cervical cancer later in life. STDs are discussed in detail in Chapter 8.

"Do any girls ever regret having sex or not holding out?"

Quickie Answer: Yes. Most, actually.

The Full Scoop: Among teens who have had sex, eight out of ten girls and six out of ten boys admit that they wish they had waited until they were older. When younger teen girls have sex, it is often unwanted or even forced.

A sad fact is that the younger a teenaged girl is when she has sex for the first time, the more likely it is that she had unwanted or possibly involuntary sex; that's rape. About four out of ten girls who had sex before the age of thirteen to fourteen report it as unwanted. Remember, at this age, even if the girls wanted to have sex, it's still considered rape, because by law, she's not old enough to consent. Read more in Chapter 5.

"Is it OK to masturbate?"

Quickie Answer: That's up to you, but it's fine with us.

The Full Scoop: Masturbation is a tough topic to talk about with your parents or other people because it is such a private thing . . . literally. Think of it as "solo" sex. To masturbate means to touch yourself in a sexual way in the genital area to create sexual pleasure that may or may not lead to orgasm. Believe it or not, even babies masturbate. Haven't you seen them put their hand right on their "privates" during a diaper change? It feels good, so it's something they discover and naturally do. It's also normal for adolescents and even adults. Keep in mind, however, that **it should be private, should not occupy all your free time, and it's not a group activity.**

For some girls, masturbation is a safe way to satisfy sexual urges without having to worry about the risks involved with having sex with a partner.

"What is mutual masturbation?"

The Full Scoop: Mutual masturbation is when two people are touching each other's genitals to create sexual pleasure for each other. Actually, this activity can be a part of "foreplay," which includes the sexual stuff a couple does that prepares their bodies for sex. It can include things like kissing and hugging, but when it involves touching the genitals with your hands, it becomes "heavy petting" or "mutual masturbation." It doesn't have to lead to sex, but often it is very arousing and makes it more difficult to stop.

Before you get involved with mutual masturbation with a partner, you need to make sure you have set your sexual boundaries and made them clear to your partner. It takes tons of self-control to stop sexual activity when you are really aroused. That's because your body is totally getting ready for "the act" and your brain has to jump in to stop it. **You can avoid these risks by not even going there or at least by having an agreement with your partner about where you will stop.** If you don't feel comfortable talking with your partner about your sexual boundaries, you definitely are not ready to do sexual stuff with him. Remember, honest communication and being true to your personal values are key in a real romantic relationship.

By the way, we know that some teens make mutual masturbation a group activity, but we really don't believe that's okay. It's way too dangerous, and it turns sex into something more like a sport than an intimate, satisfying activity between two people who care about each other.

"Is oral sex really 'sex'?"

The Full Scoop: We talk to girls all the time who wonder if oral sex "counts" as sex. Guess what? It does. Sexual intercourse may be only the penis-in-vagina thing, but sex involves that AND all the other stuff that feels good sexually. **Sex is any act that involves**

pleasuring someone's genital area (penis, vulva, vagina, anus), no matter what you use to do the pleasuring (mouth, hand, vagina, penis, object). That doesn't sound very romantic, but sometimes we just have to say it that way to get the point across. That means oral sex and anal sex are SEX; phone sex is not. It has to do with sexual pleasure *and* intimate physical contact with genital parts. You can only get pregnant from "penis-in-vagina sex," but you can definitely get sexually transmitted infections from oral and anal sex (see Chapter 8). And you can get emotionally devastated from any form of sex if it's not what you want and in the right relationship. Get real and accept the fact that these activities are sex and put you at risk for the emotional and physical consequences of penis-in-vagina sex.

We know that many teens today don't consider oral sex to be a big deal. You should probably think about that one again. Is it not intimate to have someone's face in your vulva or your mouth around a penis? Seems pretty intimate to us. Intimate behaviors belong in intimate relationships.

"If I've only had oral sex, then I'm still a virgin, right?"

Quickie Answer: Hmmmmm, what is virginity to you?

The Full Scoop: The term "virginity" gets a lot of attention, especially in some school sex ed programs. Some teens sign virginity pledges and others are encouraged by their parents and other adults to stay a virgin until marriage. It sounds like a good idea, but we know that a lot of teens consider virginity as only one thing—no penis in the vagina. That leads to something called "technical virginity," where a girl may have had oral sex, anal sex, group sex . . . all kinds of crazy sex, but never allowed a penis in her vagina. Do you think she is "sexually innocent"? That's what virginity is really about. **It's more than just keeping a penis out of the vagina.** If you remain sexually innocent, your first sexual experience will be something special that you share with the person you have grown to love, trust, and, hopefully, are committed to for a long time. If you're not concerned about "sexual innocence," then stop trying to define virginity, stay safe, and be realistic about what you're doing.

"Is oral sex safe?"

Quickie Answer: From pregnancy? Yes. From STDs? No!

The Full Scoop: It might be safe as far as preventing pregnancy, but it's not considered "safe sex" unless you are using protection in the form of a condom or other barrier to cover the genital skin. Yes, condoms should be used by girls who perform oral sex on a guy. There are actually flavored condoms for this purpose. For a guy giving a girl oral sex, he can protect his mouth and her genitals by covering the area with a split-open, nonlubricated condom or even household plastic wrap. **It may sound awkward, but if you make the choice to have oral sex, you need to be mature about it and protect yourself.**

Having oral sex can lead to infection in the mouth or throat with gonorrhea, chlamydia, syphilis, HPV and herpes. Herpes is the most common sexually transmitted infection caused by oral sex. In fact, in our offices, oral sex is the most common cause for new cases of genital herpes in teen girls. Did you know that **a common cold sore is a form of the herpes virus, and it can be transferred from the mouth to the vulva or penis very easily?** It doesn't necessarily mean that someone with a cold sore got it sexually, but the virus doesn't care where it grows as long as there's a moist environment (like a mouth, vulva, penis, anus, or even an eye). Herpes is a virus that is not curable and can cause recurrent infections over your entire lifetime.

The other scary thing is that most people may not even know when they have a cold sore or the herpes virus on their mouth or on their genital area, because the virus can be present even when there is no sore visible. In fact, it is estimated that 70 percent of genital herpes infections occur when there are no signs of an outbreak. Read more about it in Chapter 8. So if you are going to have oral sex, you need to know that unprotected oral sex is risky.

"Is it okay to swallow?"

Quickie Answer: **No. If you're referring to semen, it's actually dangerous.**

The Full Scoop: We've already mentioned all the stuff that is in semen (see page 121). To recap briefly, it contains a teaspoon or so of a bunch of sugars, enzymes, hormones, proteins, fats, cholesterol, vitamins, and, of course, 200–500 million sperm cells. More importantly, it can also carry bacteria and viruses (including HIV) that cause sexually transmitted infections. Yes, you can get an

STD in your throat and on your mouth. You could end up with ugly sores on your lips or a sore throat that just won't go away. If the sore throat is not treated, the infection can lead to skin rashes or even arthritis. We've already mentioned the importance of using a barrier to prevent STDs during oral sex. So, bottom line, swallowing semen carries the same risk for STDs as having unprotected sex. In fact, swallowing semen IS unprotected sex. And you know how stupid that is.

"My BF wants to give me oral sex, but I don't feel comfortable with it. What should I do?"

Quickie Answer: Tell him.

The Full Scoop: You should always remember that sex should be mutually pleasurable and not uncomfortable for either partner. If you are in a relationship where you are being pressured to try something that makes you feel uncomfortable, it's not a healthy relationship. **You should be able to honestly talk with your BF about your sexual boundaries, and what you like and don't like when it comes to physical contact.** If you can't discuss these things, your relationship is not even close to being ready for physical intimacy, so save yourself the regret.

It may seem nice that your BF wants to make you feel good sexually, but if you're not ready, you actually won't enjoy it. It might even make you feel guilty about doing something you don't feel ready for. For girls to feel comfortable trying new things sexually, it takes tons of trust, comfort, and security in a relationship. If your relationship isn't there yet, you won't feel good emotionally about the sexual things you're doing.

"What is 69?"

Quickie Answer: Mutual oral sex.

The Full Scoop: If you look at the shape of the 6 and the 9 and how they fit together, it gives a visual stick-figure-type image of how two people are positioned if they are giving each other oral sex at the same time. Intimate and personal? Absolutely. Remember that oral sex carries risks of getting STDs unless the couple is using barriers to prevent the transfer of bacteria.

"Is anal sex safe?"

The Full Scoop: Anal sex is more dangerous than other forms of sex because the tissues in the anal canal and rectum tear and bleed more easily than vaginal tissues. The rectum and anus are loaded with all the bacteria that live in feces (poop) so the risk of infection can be high. Also, many STDs, especially HIV and hepatitis, are transmitted through blood and semen, so the risk of infection is higher with anal sex.

"What do you recommend doing IF you have sex and are too embarrassed to tell your mom or anyone about it?"

Quickie Answer: **Keep trying to find your voice to speak up to someone.**

The Full Scoop: Being embarrassed and having regrets or confusion about having sex are amazingly common among teen girls. And talking to your mom about it? If you're like most girls, that's hard because you worry about getting in trouble or disappointing your parents. Face it. Your parents probably don't want you having sex as a teen because they know how it can make you confused, hurt you emotionally, put you at risk for life-threatening infections, and change your life, not just from pregnancy, but also in the way it can affect your future relationships.

But if you are confused, hurt, pregnant, or emotionally devastated, who would help you the most? Probably a parent or one of the other adults in your life. Being a parent is not easy either. All good parents want the best life for their kids. But most good parents recognize that everyone makes mistakes, even their own children. And they love you anyway. That perfect life may need to be put on hold for a while to deal with real life. Disappointment and anger may be their first emotions, but love usually wins out. And they come to your side to help you rise above your problems and hopefully learn from them.

If you are having major regrets or embarrassment, maybe that's exactly what you need to say. At least that shows you've thought about what you did and you're trying to learn from it.

If you absolutely cannot discuss this issue with your mom, then finding another adult you trust to talk it over with can be really helpful. They can help you with health care, and they can help you figure out what you plan to do next. You may decide sexual abstinence is best for you right now. You may plan to continue having sex and you need help getting birth control. Either way, a trusted adult who loves you can be the most helpful and honest person in the world to help you figure it out. You just have to trust that they only want what's best for you.

Think It Through

Think It Through

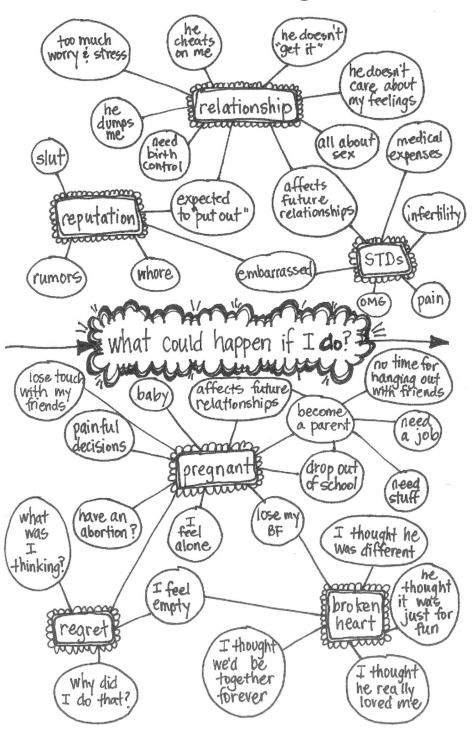

Think It Through

Chapter

5

"What happens when sex is used in the wrong way?"

The scary side of sex

A Real-Life Dilemma

"Oh. My. Gosh," Tasha murmured for the fifth time in a row, her ebony eyes wide and fixated on the glossy hardwood of the gymnasium.

Amanda was beginning to wonder if she was ever going to blink again. "Tasha, please say something besides, 'Oh my gosh.'" She'd never seen her like this, a girl who was always in control, never rattled. It was hard to know what to say, especially considering the circumstances. Chelsea and Sydney sat against the wall, passing an odd look of panic between each other. Panic situations were not what they did best.

"Maybe it's not as bad as you think?" Chelsea finally offered, cueing up her best "Go Team!" smile. "You haven't seen the video, Tash. Maybe kids are making way too much out of it."

Tasha's hollow eyes ticked toward Chelsea's hopeful expression. "Chelsea," she snapped, "my cousin made a lesbian porn video with two of her friends. It was on the Internet. How much worse can it get than that?"

Amanda edged closer. "But still, Tasha, if you haven't seen it . . ."

"My parents saw it. I swear, from the look on my mother's face, you would have thought somebody had been murdered."

"Might be, when your aunt and uncle get through with Danielle," Chelsea said.

"That's not helping, Chel," Amanda shot back. "But maybe she's right; maybe the video isn't as wild as they say. You know how parents overreact to everything."

Sydney gulped, offering up the same guilty look as the day she confessed to having sex with Aidan Scofield. "Um, guys, I sort of saw it—the video. It's pretty gross, Dani and two of her friends making out, touching each other and stuff. Sorry, Tasha, but I thought you'd rather hear it from me." Tasha closed her eyes and nodded.

Chelsea leaned in farther, whispering, "I heard they staged it just like a porn movie, wore sexy lingerie and everything."

Tasha's hands flew over her face. "Oh, no. Oh, my gosh," came a muffled groan.

"There she goes again," Amanda said. "Oh-my-gosh, what?" Reaching over, Amanda pried Tasha's hands from her face.

"The lingerie is mine . . . I loaned it to her," Tasha said.

"Since when do you own hot lingerie?" Chelsea asked. "No offense, Tasha, but you are kind of a blue jeans sort of girl."

"Yeah, I've never seen you sleep in anything but an old T-shirt," Sydney added.

"I bought it last summer. Dani and I were in this little boutique at the beach. She dared me and, well, I took the dare. When she asked to borrow it, I figured she wanted to model it for Derek, her boyfriend.

I told her I didn't want to know! But I had no idea . . ."

"Wow, so that makes you what? The wardrobe mistress," murmured Chelsea.

"Still not helping!" Amanda said, shooting her a shut-your-mouth glare. Chelsea was funny and sweet, but sometimes her mouth got ahead of her brain. "Don't worry, Tasha. Nobody will ever know that besides us. Right, Chelsea?" Pursing her lips tightly, Chelsea obediently nodded.

"Doesn't matter; everybody knows about the video," Tasha said, resting her head against the wall. "It's all over school. At first I thought I was just being paranoid, but everywhere I go, it's stares and whispers. I don't know how Dani is ever going to show her face again."

Amanda had to agree with that. Word of the x-rated, seven-minute flick only broke yesterday. But by eight o'clock last night, it was all anyone was texting anyone else about. She was tempted to look, but for Tasha's sake, Amanda didn't visit YouTube. But she heard it had about 800 hits before it was taken off that morning. "Have you talked to Dani? I don't get how something like this happens. I don't know Danielle like I know you, but she seems so . . . so normal."

"And besides that, she has boyfriend! So it's not like she goes that way. And neither do the other girls, as far as I know. What I don't get is why?" Sydney said, feigning a dramatic shiver, as though she couldn't quite get the picture out of her head. "Were they just, like, experimenting?"

"No, not according to what Dani said. I talked to her last night," said Tasha. I guess I'm the only person her parents are letting her speak to at the moment. She explained her side of it."

There was an uncomfortable silence as they all looked from one to the other and Amanda wondered if she should push it. Of course, Chelsea had no qualms. "So are you going to tell us, or what?"

"She did it because of Derek. He's been pressuring her to have sex, but she doesn't want to. So he told her if she didn't want to, he could suggest some other ways to keep his attention. He told her that seeing girls with girls was a total turn-on. I mean, why do guys think that's so hot? That's when Dani came up with this idea. She thought it was safer than actually having sex with him."

"Her own boyfriend? Gosh, I don't think even Aidan would want a girl to do that," Sydney said with a sigh. "You know, I read about something like this happening at a school in Texas. Some girls made a sex video and sent it to a teacher they thought was hot. But just like Dani, somehow it ended up on the Internet."

"What happened to them?" Tasha asked.

"Um, I think because they sent a copy to school, they all got expelled. I don't suppose Dani will be that lucky."

"I think you're right, Syd. My aunt and uncle are already talking about moving. She'll never live it down. I'll be lucky if I do! Thank God they took it off the site. I just can't believe she'd be so stupid! Dani destroyed her reputation and self-respect, not to mention the humiliation. And for what?"

Amanda filled in with what they were all surely thinking: "Because she wanted to hang on to a guy who obviously had no respect for her in the first place. Anybody who cares about you would never ask you to do something like that. Well, with any luck at all, it will all blow over."

"I hope you're right. Listen, I've got to go. My mom wanted me home right after school today." Tasha's tall frame unfolded from the gymnasium floor. "I'll talk to you guys later." She headed out the side door without another word.

"Do you think it will . . . blow over soon?" Chelsea asked. Amanda shrugged as a few boys, oblivious to the three of them, gathered in the corner. There was a quick exchange of cash and disks.

Then, like rats, they all scurried away, one boy bragging to another, "Taking that off YouTube was the best thing that could have happened. When we're done selling this skin flick to every guy at Lakeside, we'll take copies over to Tri-Valley High."

Amanda expelled a deep breath. "Well, Chel, I think there's your answer."

Doc Talk:
The Way **We See It**

DID WE MENTION YET THAT SEX IS POWERFUL? Well, that's what a lot of people believe anyway. That's the bad side of sex. And often, the stupid side of sex. Sex and sexy images are often used to sell products, provide entertainment, grab people's attention, scare people, and gain control over people. **When sex is used as a way to gain power over someone else, it's absolutely, without a doubt, unquestionably wrong.** But it happens. And it makes a lot of people do stupid things, feel horrible about themselves, and even ruin their lives.

Do you think these girls ever intended for anyone but Dani's boyfriend to see the video? Probably not. Do you think they even thought about what could go wrong as a result of making the video? Probably not. Did they remember that every single thing that is digitally created (like cell phone photos, videos, and even e-mails, voice mails, and text messages) is recordable, reproducible, and positively permanent? Nope. Instead, they thought it was a great idea to prove a point—something exciting and risky. But they never dreamed exactly how risky.

These girls have unfortunately learned a horrible lesson. They and their families have been embarrassed and humiliated. And who knows how this will affect their futures? As far as "sex and power" go, their "soft pornography" video may not seem nearly as bad as some of the other things that fall into the same category, such as rape, sexual harassment, and prostitution, but, like other horrible things, it will continue to haunt them for weeks, months, and possibly even years.

We hope to convince you that sex should never be used for power. But you're not the one we worry about the most. It's all the people "out there" who use sex to gain control over YOU that worry us most. Be aware of your rights. Know what to do if someone is sexually harassing you, if you experience rape, if pornography is affecting your life, and even if you find yourself being drawn into sexual things because YOU feel powerful. There are a lot of resources out there to help in all of these circumstances. The most important first step is to ask for help. If you have more questions that aren't answered here, please e-mail them to us through our website (www.girlology.com) and look for the answers there.

YOU Asked!

"Why are so many guys into porn?"

Quickie Answer: It's everywhere, it's shocking, and it's addictive.

The Full Scoop: Pornography is so easy to access these days because of the Internet. It can pop up on your computer even when you're not looking for it. Once you see it, it catches your attention and curiosity takes over. Guys buy and view porn a lot more often than girls do. It probably goes back to the thing about guys seeing sex as more physical and girls seeing it on a more emotional level. Some guys even get addicted to porn because they start to depend on it for sexual arousal. Girls don't seem to develop porn "addictions," but some view it because they are very curious, and sometimes they just want to appease their BF.

There are more cases of porn addiction because it has become so available on the Internet, TV, videos, and magazines. Keep in mind that there's a big difference between talking about it and actually spending a lot of time watching it. Your BF may just talk about it because his friends laugh and he likes the attention. But if your BF seems obsessed with watching it, then he may have an addiction that can lead to major relationship and personal problems in the future.

Pornography is horrible for many reasons. **It takes sex out of the proper context of being a normal and healthy way for mature adults to express their love to one another.** The other thing that bothers us about pornography is that it is degrading to women and it cheapens sex. Porn often shows women as victims or possessions, not equal partners in the relationship. It also portrays very unrealistic and abnormal sexual scenarios and behaviors. **And besides all that, it's totally lame.** The story lines are ridiculous, the acting is pitiful, and the scenarios are incredibly unrealistic.

Research has shown that men who view porn are more likely to accept violence against women, are sexually insensitive, are more aggressive toward women, and have little compassion for women as rape victims. Doesn't sound like the type of guy you're looking for, does it? Porn makes sex seem more like a spectator sport rather than the intimate and fulfilling thing that it really is in the right relationship.

"My BF and his buddies talk about how hot it is to watch girls have sex with each other. Why do they think that's hot?"

The Full Scoop: Actually, if a guy sees anything sexual, he will probably think it's hot. Teens tend to get excited about things that are shocking to others, like sex between lesbians. Even in some of the underage, no-alcohol-allowed teen clubs, some girls make out with each other or dance erotically with each other to entertain the guys. It's that let-me-try-to-shock-you-and-control-you, bad power thing again. Some make it their goal to create a bigger and better shock factor. Sometimes just talking about something shocking makes guys feel cool. **Sex is not meant to be a spectator sport, so watching anyone have sex, no matter what "type" of sex it is, is not normal.** Guys may talk about how hot it is to watch, but if your BF feels the need to watch something like that to get sexually aroused, then he needs psychological help.

Remember the red flag stuff? Well, a true interest in porn is another one, and you need to let your BF know that you don't want any part of it. Trying to figure out how to say it without sounding like a prude? For the guy who wants you to watch porn with him, you could reply with, "Sex is not a spectator sport." And for the guy who likes to watch porn, try, "Too bad you need to rent your dates; I prefer mine to be real." Or maybe it doesn't even deserve a response from you. Don't waste your breath. Just roll your eyes and leave. Chances are, he may never be able to relate to a girl in the real world.

"I just saw a picture of me looking drunk and stupid on my friend's boyfriend's MySpace page. How can I get it off?"

Quickie Answer: You can't.

The Full Scoop: One of the biggest challenges that teens face today is learning how to live in the digital world where anywhere, anytime, anyone can click your photo into their cell phone and have it all over the Internet within minutes. It could be something as innocent as posing with your family in front of the Grand Canyon or as incriminating as taking a hit off of a beer bong, hanging out with someone else's BF, or much, much worse. It's scary to think that you have to watch your behavior so carefully, but you do, especially at parties and around other teens. Remember that pretty much everything you do is recordable, reproducible, and can get "out there" really fast.

"My teacher keeps texting me sexual jokes. It grosses me out. How can I make him stop?"

Quickie Answer: It sounds like sexual harassment, and it's illegal.

The Full Scoop: A lot of girls are flattered by flirting. It's welcomed attention, and it's usually playful and fun. But it's never okay for an adult in a position of authority (teacher, coach, leader, boss) to flirt with a teen—that crosses the line into the realm of sexual harassment.

Sexual harassment can be a lot of things, but it involves sexually charged comments or actions that make you feel uncomfortable. Some examples include unwanted touching, telling sexually explicit jokes, sending text messages or e-mails with sexual content, making sexual suggestions, or even looking at you or gesturing in a way that implies sexual desire and makes you feel uncomfortable.

The most important thing to know about sexual harassment is that it is illegal and you can definitely do something about it.

If you experience something like this from a peer, you should first try to tell the person who is doing it to stop. If they don't stop, then it's time to go to an adult, such as a counselor, teacher, or your parent. When it's a teacher, a boss, or another adult doing the harassing, it can be even more difficult. Then you need to go to another adult to get help. Your parents may be the best place to start. They can help you address the problem at school.

By law, all schools have sexual harassment policies that protect you and help everyone understand the rules. Your guidance counselor, another teacher, or your principal can work with you and your parents to resolve the problem.

Reporting sexual harassment is important because **nobody has the right to use sex and sexual things to make you feel uncomfortable.** If you don't report it, it is very likely that the harasser will keep harassing you and probably many others, too. Behaviors like that are not acceptable and need to be corrected. If you tell an adult and they don't take you seriously, or don't help you take steps to change the situation, you will need to talk with someone else. Keep working to end the harassment. It can be a frustrating problem to try to change, but a change like this is important for you and for the other girls and women who may encounter the harasser in the future.

"What exactly is rape?"

Quickie Answer: It's a crime no matter what the circumstance.

The Full Scoop: Rape (also called sexual assault) occurs when someone is forced or coerced (talked into it by threatening them) into having sex: oral sex, anal sex, or vaginal sex. Most rapes are committed by guys the victim knows; most victims are teen girls and young adult women, and most rapes happen in someone's home (or apartment or dorm). It is not the stranger-in-a-dark-alley scene that most girls think of.

If a guy forces his penis, finger, tongue, or other object into a female's vagina or anus, it's sexual assault. If a guy forces a girl to have oral sex with him, it is also sexual assault. Using "force" doesn't necessarily mean there is always physical force, but the "force" might be less obvious. That's what can make it confusing. It's still considered rape if a guy talks a girl into having sex when she really doesn't want to. Or if he threatens to spread rumors about her if she doesn't. Or if he uses his authority over her (that would be like if he has some power over her as her teacher, boss, coach, religious leader, or relative) to talk her into it. If a guy has sex with a girl who is drunk, high, or unconscious, it is rape because she is not able to consent to sex. **Giving consent means saying "yes" and knowing what you are saying.** If you say he should stop, no matter how far you've gone, he needs to stop. If you are drunk or high, your judgment is impaired, and legally you can't give consent.

If you've experienced some sort of sexual act that was against your will, it was rape. It can make you feel confused; it can make you feel bad about yourself; and it might even make you feel partially to blame because you weren't clear about saying no. **The truth is that nobody has the right to have sex with you unless you clearly say you want it.** If you've experienced a sexual assault by a boyfriend, a stranger, or an acquaintance, it's important to get medical attention and to talk with someone who can help. Your local rape crisis center is a good place to start. You can also call the National Rape Abuse and Incest Hotline at 1-800-656-HOPE or visit their website at www.rainn.org.

If you ever experience a rape in the future, you need to report it as soon as possible to the police or an adult who can help. Your first step would be to call 911 and go to your local rape crisis center or emergency room (ER). Getting medical attention is important to make sure you don't have injuries and that you receive medications to prevent pregnancy and STDs. If you report it to the police, they will request that the nurse or doctor collect evidence from your body to help them identify the person who raped you. The evidence will be collected during your physical exam. To increase the chances of finding evidence of the rape, it's important that you don't shower, bathe, go to the bathroom, brush your teeth, or change clothing before you go to the ER. A rape crisis counselor will usually be there to help you understand the process and to be a friend through the process. She will make sure you know where to get the help you will need to heal, both emotionally and physically.

It may seem scary to report the rape, especially if the rapist is your boyfriend or someone you know. What you need to know is that most guys who do this once will do it again and again. By speaking up, you might be helping another girl avoid a similar trauma in the future.

"My dad said he'll call the police if my BF and I have sex. Can the police really do anything?"

Quickie Answer: Yes, if you are under the age of consent in your state.

The Full Scoop: Every state has something called an "age of consent." That's the age you have to be to legally consent to sex. Different states have different ages, but they range from fifteen to eighteen. For example, let's assume your state's age of consent is seventeen and you are sixteen. That means that even if you have sex because you want to, your consent doesn't count because you're not old enough, and your partner can be prosecuted for statutory rape. Statutory rape means someone has had sex with a person who is legally too young to have sex. Another form of statutory rape is when someone in a position of authority (like a teacher, a coach, or a boss) has sex with a minor. The bottom line is that when you're young, adult men and men in positions of authority over you cannot have sex with you. Even if you agree, it's still a form of rape. And yes, your dad could call the police and press charges, and so could you. If you are both under the age of consent, the guy can still be arrested. The charges are usually less severe if the involved teens are close in age. The wider the gap between their ages, the harsher the consequences or punishment.

"I love him, but I wasn't ready for sex. Was it rape?"

Quickie Answer: Unless you said yes, it was rape.

The Full Scoop: Many girls who experience rape are confused about whether it was really rape. When you have romantic feelings for your BF and you're involved sexually without having intercourse, sometimes your guy can get pushy and talk you into going further than you want. If you say "yes" to sex when you don't mean it, you've given him the wrong message. If you don't say anything at all, he can easily interpret that as a "yes." That's why it's so important to find your voice and firmly say "stop." It's not easy, but you have to do it. **You can't rely on body language, like moving his hands away, closing your legs, or turning away. Guys need clear messages.** Instead, you have to say, "I don't want to go any further" or "I need to stop, now." A guy who respects you will honor your request and stop. If he doesn't or if he tries to talk you out of it, he's not respecting your boundaries. That can lead to rape. Rape sounds like a harsh word for something that happens between you and your BF, but that's exactly what it is. Sex is such a big deal that it requires both partners to be totally agreeable to everything that happens. That's why consent is required, even by law.

A great way to prevent this type of situation is to **be clear about your sexual boundaries before you get physically intimate or at least shortly after the kissing starts.** If your BF doesn't honor your boundaries or doesn't take you seriously, consider it one of those red flags. It's time to get out of that relationship. In a healthy relationship, he'll respect you. You'll find that clear communication will build trust and keep you away from painful experiences like this.

"How can I avoid date rape?"

The Full Scoop: Although a girl who is raped is not to blame and she often can't stop it, there are things that can decrease the chances that a date rape will happen. Some of these strategies are related to alcohol, and they are listed in Chapter 6.

The following strategies may keep you from becoming a victim of date rape in the future, even when alcohol is not an issue.

* Do not accept a ride home from any guy who you don't know well and trust completely. Even then, you should avoid being alone in a car with a guy you've just met or don't know well.

* If you're going out with someone new, plan to meet him at a place where there are plenty of other people around, and have your own transportation.

* Never go alone to a guy's home, apartment, dorm room, and so on. Make sure you have a friend along with you or that a responsible adult is present to supervise. It's sad to think that being alone with a guy is always risky, but it can be.

* Never be the only girl among a group of guys.

* If a guy is getting physically aggressive with you, immediately leave the area if you can. You don't need to offer any explanation. If you can't get away from him, yell for help and clearly tell him to stop. Using your own physical force as you try to get away can also be effective.

* Listen to your "gut instincts." If you don't feel safe, get away from the situation.

* If you're going to a party (and, really, anywhere you go), you should always try to have a friend with you.

* Keep your cell phone with you if you are on a date or at a party or any other function where guys are around. Call for help if you need it.

It's sad to think that girls have to be so cautious, but date rape is common and can be very traumatic. Be safe. Be smart. Be alert.

"There's a guy at school who keeps telling me he wants to hook up with me. I like him, but what does he mean by 'hook up'?"

Quickie Answer: It could mean anything from meeting up with him to chat or meeting up for nothing but casual sex.

The Full Scoop: The term "hook-up" has become popular in today's culture as a term to describe casual sex. Among teens and young adults, it has become **a popular excuse for getting sexual desires fulfilled with no emotional attachment.** Sometimes hook-ups involve people who are friends, sometimes strangers hook up after nothing more than a brief introduction or Internet chat. People who are into hooking up probably have had multiple partners, and there's no way to know how responsible they have been with trying to prevent diseases.

Hook-ups are tremendously risky, both physically and emotionally. The physical risk is obvious. Having sex with a stranger or multiple partners can expose you to every disease in the book. Among teens, condom use is actually more common with hook-ups than in long-term relationships. But condoms are not 100 percent effective, so your risks for HIV, HPV, herpes, and other STDs are extremely high.

It's hard to separate sex from your emotions, but that's exactly what hook-ups try to do. For girls especially, sex creates emotional attachments that are hard to break, no matter how much you try to convince yourself otherwise. Girls are wired to want emotional intimacy and security before we become physically intimate. Most girls are also brought up to believe that sex is part of an intimate, committed relationship; it's hard to abolish that belief.

Lots of girls will agree to a hook-up but then find themselves feeling more attached to the guy than they intended. That leaves them feeling used and hurt when he moves on. But there weren't supposed to be any strings attached, right? Save yourself the pain. Most girls just aren't "wired" that way. Remember that in a healthy relationship, you will develop **emotional intimacy before physical intimacy. Hook-ups turn it completely around.** It's just backward. Although a hook-up might be a way for a relationship to start, it's starting in a very unhealthy way.

On the other hand, there are some girls who will initiate hook-ups because it gives them a sense of power. We all know that sex is powerful—in both good and bad ways. And some guys will do *anything* to have sex. That gives these girls a real sense of control. Some girls will try hooking up to satisfy their need to feel wanted by a guy. Some hook up because they feel a thrill from it. Some girls can even become "addicted" to the control and power they feel with hook-ups. Most of these girls have grown up in conditions where they felt powerless, unloved, and out of control. The power they feel with hook-ups makes them feel good for a while, but it's no solution. Most girls like this will benefit from professional help, which allows them to accept themselves and begin to heal from past experiences.

So, back to your question. You need to ask him exactly what he means by "hook-up." If he wants a no-strings-attached sex hook-up, forget it. You already said you really like him, so you won't be able to separate your emotions from the hook-up. You'll just end up feeling pain, jealousy, or regret. If he just wants to hook up to hang out, then great. Have fun. Just make sure you stay smart and communicate well.

So how do you respond when your dream date ends up wanting nothing more than a hook-up? First of all, don't worry about hurting his feelings. Just make your point. How about saying something like, "Let me get this straight. You want me to put out without getting to know me? Without buying me flowers? Making me dinner? Rubbing my feet and running barefoot on the beach? Finding out what I like and don't like? Well, guess what? I don't like that. So my answer would be no." It may not all be true, but it will definitely get your point across. You could also try something short and sweet, like, "Who are you? No thanks," or, "Better luck next time. I'm not into that." And there's always plain and simple, "No!" No need for apologies or excuses from you. Requests like that don't deserve it.

Think It Through

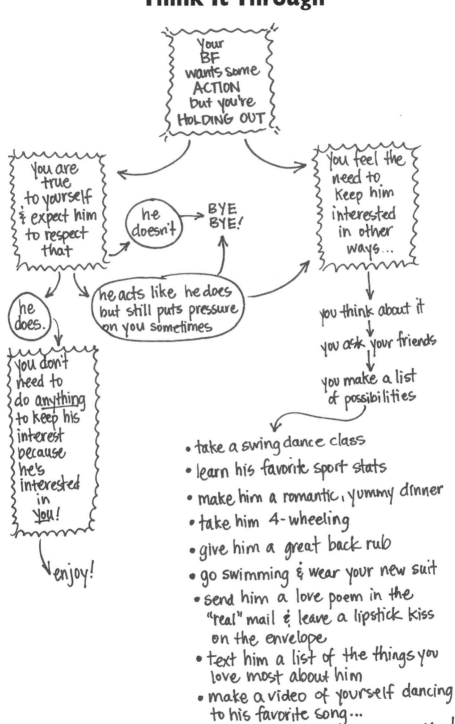

Your BF wants some ACTION but you're HOLDING OUT

You are true to yourself & expect him to respect that

he doesn't → BYE BYE!

You feel the need to keep him interested in other ways...

he does.

he acts like he does but still puts pressure on you sometimes

you think about it

you ask your friends

you make a list of possibilities

You don't need to do anything to keep his interest because he's interested in you!

enjoy!

- take a swing dance class
- learn his favorite sport stats
- make him a romantic, yummy dinner
- take him 4-wheeling
- give him a great back rub
- go swimming & wear your new suit
- send him a love poem in the "real" mail & leave a lipstick kiss on the envelope
- text him a list of the things you love most about him
- make a video of yourself dancing to his favorite song...
  a video? great idea... a video!!

Think It Through

Think It Through

Beware of what's recorded...

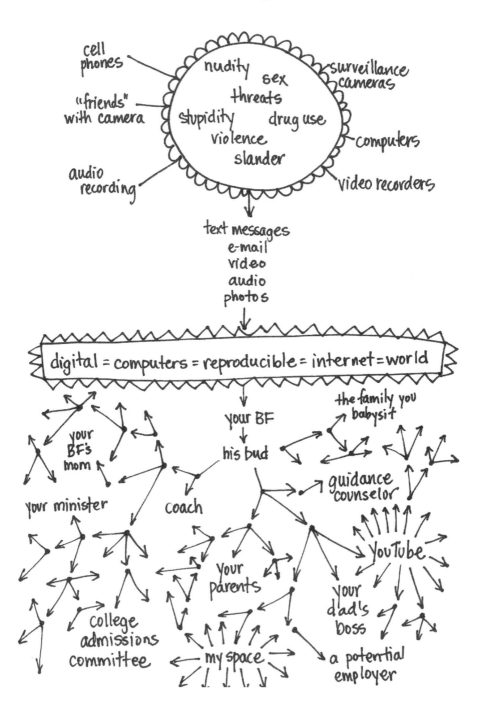

Chapter

6

"It's not really a drug, is it?"

Alcohol and sex don't mix well

A Real-Life Dilemma

Tasha's car pulled to the curb, a few doors down from Shelby Renner's house. It was only 9:30, but from the line of cars and steady thrum of music, it looked and sounded as if the party had been going on for hours. Why not? There was free beer and a very promising rumor that the boys' basketball team was going to show. Still, Tasha could see Chelsea's hesitant expression, examining the scene like a house of horrors.

"Come on, Chelsea. What's the big deal? Look, I know you're not into the whole drinking thing, but this is a great party—no parents, older brother home from college, and a keg. We're lucky we got the invite."

"Yeah, I guess. It's just that, well, if my mom knew . . ."

"Uh, Chel, your mom needs to get a clue," Tasha said, fishing through her purse for lip gloss. "Kids are going to drink." She tilted the rearview mirror, applying a third coat to already iridescent lips. "Think of it this way. Shelby's brother, Sam—he's, like, providing a community service, a safe place to party."

Not looking terribly convinced, Chelsea glanced between Tasha and the house. "Still . . . if I get caught . . . my mom's not like yours. I mean, your mom's a doctor. She sees it all. She gets it, everything kids do nowadays, drinking and stuff. Mine's not quite so in the loop," she said with a roll of her eyes. "But your mom is way cool. I'm pretty sure she wouldn't kill you."

"Mmm, well, I don't know if I'd go that far," Tasha laughed, smacking her freshly painted lips. "Listen, let's just go in. If you're not having a blast in like an hour, we'll leave."

"Together?" she asked, her big green eyes bugging out a little farther than usual.

"Yeah, we'll stick together—promise."

• • •

Two hours into the party, Tasha realized she'd lost track of Chelsea. It was easy to do. Invited or not, most of Lakeside High's junior class had showed up. Tasha wanted to find her just to say: *I told you so.* It *was* an awesome party. And Sam seemed in charge. He'd even broken up a nasty catfight on the front lawn. No surprise there. Kristen Shaw had it coming, making out with Dawn Antinelli's boyfriend in the Renner's guest room. What a slut, Tasha thought, heading down the basement steps on a hunt for Chelsea.

The room swayed to the pounding of loud rap. Or maybe it was just swaying period. Tasha giggled, weaving through the crowd, scanning for her friend. Everybody was there. Well, everybody who was close to being anybody. A strong hand grasped her shoulder, nearly spinning her off balance.

"Tasha! Hey, girl, I didn't know you were here?"

She forced a mouthful of beer down her throat, having come face-to-face with Ty Johnson: basketball star and one of the hottest guys at school. He had this effect on her: speechlessness, loss of muscle tone, weak-kneed. Tasha would give just about anything for him to even notice her. "Hey there, Ty," Tasha said, flashing her biggest smile, hoping that at least one coat of lip-gloss was still intact. "Great party, huh?"

"Yeah, it's all right," he slurred, downing the last of his beer. "We've been here a while though. A couple of us were thinking about headin' out. Wanna come?"

"Me? Um, sure," she gulped, watching his make-your-mouth-water, six-two frame wobble just a bit. "But I can't go until I find Chelsea. You know, Chelsea Knowles, I came with her."

"Whatever," he said, smacking the hand of kids who passed—like a rock star. "Let me know." Someone offered another beer and he took it, turning toward a different conversation.

She had to find Chelsea—fast! No doubt she'd be glad for an excuse to go. Chelsea would have never even agreed to the party if Zach, her stuck-like-glue boyfriend, hadn't gone out of town. Elbowing her way through the crowd, Tasha finally spied her. At least she thought it was Chelsea, laughing loudly with some older guys Tasha didn't know. "Um, Chel, what the hell are you doing?"

"Tasha!" she gushed. "You were so right! This is the best freakin' party." Raising the plastic cup to her mouth, a dribble of beer dripped down her chin. "Do you know Mark?" A shaggy-looking guy with a sly grin waved, his arm slung around Chelsea's shoulder. "He's Sam's college mate . . ." she giggled. "I mean, college roommate."

"Oh, Chelsea, how . . . how much have you had to drink?" she demanded, guilt drowning out her own beer buzz. It should have been a red alert when Chelsea disappeared. Without her own crowd or Zach, she'd be likely to follow the lead of anyone who wanted to tell her what to do. It was just like Chelsea to go along with whatever when left on her own.

"The guys here, they've been like *sooo* nice. They taught me the coolest game. Beer Pong. I can never seem to get that little ball in the cup. See, he got another one in before I did," she announced loudly, swinging the cup high.

With the next whoosh of her arm, Chelsea lost her balance, toppling into Tasha. "Yeah, Chel, you win or lose?" Just as she steadied her friend, Tasha saw Ty heading right for her, the smell of beer arriving just ahead of him.

"Tasha, we're outta here. You comin'?" He crushed his empty cup and sent it sailing in a perfect arc toward the trashcan, where it bounced off the rim. "Damn, that was a nothin' shot, too."

Tasha looked apprehensively at Chelsea, who was now using Mark as furniture, her entire body draped across him. The beer in her own stomach sloshed, glancing at the gorgeous but clearly wasted Ty Johnson. It would be stupid to go with him, but twice as stupid to let him drive. How was she supposed to stop him? He'd laugh in her face. He'd never want anything to do with her if she tried to keep him from leaving.

Nuzzling Chelsea's blonde head, Mark yelled over the music, "Hey, if you want to take off, I'll look after your friend. No problem."

The way his arm wrapped tight around Chelsea's rag doll body made Tasha's skin crawl. "Um, no thanks, that's okay," Tasha said, jerking Chelsea away from him and watching her slump to the floor.

"Tasha, the guys are waitin'. It's now or never, girl," Ty said, playfully tossing his keys in the air.

Tasha surprised herself, catching the keys midflight, quickly tucking them inside her sweater. If he tried to recover them, it would be a small consolation on the night. "You're not driving anywhere. You're drunk. You can get them back tomorrow." Tasha swallowed hard and waited for the backlash, staring at Ty's awestruck expression.

But maybe he was too drunk to get angry, because Ty's only response was, "Damn," as he rubbed a hand around his neck, staring back at her. "You are one very in-control girl."

Tasha wasn't sure if that was good or bad. It didn't matter at the moment, as she turned her attention to Chelsea, who was more than wasted. She looked dangerously close to puking or passing out— probably both. Tasha thought about Ashley Scott. She once drank so much at a party she almost died of alcohol poisoning. It was Tasha's own mother who'd pumped the girl's stomach in the emergency room. Hopefully, Chelsea wasn't that far gone, but she couldn't be sure. With a deep breath, Tasha pulled out her cell. "Well, like you said, Chel, I'm pretty sure she won't kill me."

Doc Talk:
The Way **We See It**

WE COULD WRITE AN ENTIRE BOOK ON drugs and alcohol, but we'll try to keep this chapter short and to the point. We address the topic in this book because **drugs and alcohol are so closely related to sexual activity among teens.** We know that most teens experiment with alcohol, but sometimes it's regular use or abuse. However much it is, there is no doubt that using drugs and alcohol will cloud your ability to make good decisions or affect your life in some other serious way.

Way too many teens get drunk or even buzzed and then lose their virginity or have sex when they don't really want to. Having sex under the influence of alcohol makes you less likely to insist on condom use or even think about birth control.

It's also important to remember that when girls are high or wasted, guys notice. And it's not the type of attention you want. Some guys are just looking for a drunk girl. It's the perfect setup for a date rape. It's sad to think there are guys like that out there, but there are. Some may act that way because of alcohol's influence, and some just are that way.

As doctors, we have to be understanding, but **we want to send a clear message that drugs and alcohol are not appropriate for teens.** There are several reasons why. First of all, it's illegal. Breaking the law is the kind of thing that ends up on your "permanent record." Having an arrest on your record can follow you and keep you from realizing your goals (they even throw people off reality TV shows for convictions like that). Second, science is discovering more and more about the teen brain and its development. It's becoming very clear that alcohol and drugs can result in permanent changes in the structure and abilities of your brain. Who needs a short circuit when you're just figuring out how to get it together? Finally, it messes up your judgment. And this is at a time in your life when you need all the help you can get making good decisions. That means you end up taking risks you wouldn't take otherwise. Ultimately, that leads to trouble and regret.

Be smart about alcohol and drug use. Know how to say no. Know what these substances do, and what they don't do. For starters, they don't improve your life (not even your sex life). Ever.

"I'm going to a party this week-end and I know there will be alcohol. How do I say no?"

Quickie Answer: Plan your strategy now before you go.

The Full Scoop: First, let's talk about why teens drink. Most admit to trying alcohol because they are curious about how it makes them feel. Others admit that they drink to feel buzzed, relax, or reduce stress in their lives. Still others admit to drinking in order to fit in or feel older. Peer pressure may have a lot to do with it. Even though your friends might not encourage you to take a drink, seeing them drink makes you feel like you should. If you're drinking along with them, you don't feel left out. Remember how we mentioned that the stuff you're around a lot starts to seem normal? Being around a lot of underage drinking makes you think it's normal. It's not. Don't be fooled.

So how you can say no? Here are a few ideas to try. It helps if you **have a plan before someone puts a drink in your hand.** You might even want to practice "your lines" at home. It will be easier if you have said it to yourself a few times—even in a mirror.

Let your parents take the hit. Blame them or another adult. Say something like, "My dad is picking me up soon and I don't want him to smell it on me." Or "I am already on restriction for something else. If I get caught drinking, I can kiss my car good-bye." How about, "My coach will kill me if she finds out. We have a big game tomorrow." Putting the blame on someone else may make it easier for you. Or a simple yet firm response can often avoid follow-up questions. How about, "I have a big event [or game] tomorrow and I want to do my best," or even, "I got so sick last time I drank, I'm taking a break." Having a strategy with a friend is also helpful. Develop a signal that means you are ready to leave, but make sure you are both willing to follow through.

If you don't drink, and you have the confidence to just be yourself, then say no thanks. No further explanation needed. You can still hang out and have fun. Sometimes others will even respect you for that and stop offering alcohol or pressuring you to drink. That's when it pays off to be yourself.

If you and your friends don't drink, you'll find the parties with alcohol can be boring or stupid, and you'll have a better time with others who are sober. Plus, you'll have a clear head and remember all the fun you had. Another plus is that you'll have no worries about stupid remarks or rumor-starting behaviors that happened because of the effects of alcohol.

"How much alcohol is safe for me to drink?"

The Full Scoop: The first thing to remember is that if you're under age twenty-one, it's illegal. So it's obviously not safe for your character and your future goals to have an arrest on your record. On the other hand, you probably see teens use alcohol without obvious problems from it. You may hear your friends say that alcohol makes them feel more relaxed. Some people lose inhibitions and seem friendly and talkative. Some become more aggressive or even angry. Others just look and act plain stupid.

In reality, alcohol is a depressant that slows the function of your brain. In small amounts, **it actually blocks important messages that are trying to get to your brain.** This can decrease your coordination and impair your judgment. In larger amounts it slows your reflexes, slurs your speech, messes up your vision, causes you to have memory lapses, and even causes you to have blackouts.

Another important thing to remember is that females don't metabolize alcohol as quickly as males do. So for girls, alcohol gets in the bloodstream faster and stays there longer than it does for guys. That means girls get drunk faster and stay drunk longer than guys. How fast you get drunk also depends on your body weight and how much food is in your stomach to slow down the absorption of the alcohol. For teen girls, just one or two drinks will put your blood alcohol content in the impaired to legally drunk range. But if you're not driving, does it matter? It does.

Alcohol use has been shown to have permanent effects on growing brain cells. It also leads to unintended and unsafe sexual behaviors and rape. Among teens, alcohol use is associated with poor school performance, depression, alcoholism as an adult, and higher rates of injuries, accidental death, and suicide. So how much is safe? There's no safe answer. If you can wait until your brain is finished developing (around twenty-one!), then learn to drink responsibly, you'll save yourself from many problems and you'll maintain your amazing brain power.

"I was drinking at a party last weekend and I woke up at my friend's house without my underwear. I don't remember what happened."

Quickie Answer: You had a blackout. It could have been from too much alcohol or from being drugged.

The Full Scoop: Blacking out occurs most commonly after consuming a large amount of alcohol over a short period of time. But it can also happen with a small amount of alcohol mixed with one of the date rape drugs or other potent drugs.

If you blacked out from drinking too much alcohol, it's time to get real about your drinking habits. Getting drunk is not an admirable goal for anyone. Most teens don't think about the negative sides of getting wasted, like vomiting, blackouts, loss of memory, severely impaired judgment, and hangovers. The impaired judgment part is the scariest because that's when teens make really stupid mistakes like driving, having unprotected sex, unwanted sex, fighting with friends, and so on. And they often don't even remember what they did. Talk about worry?! Blacking out is also one of the signs of alcohol poisoning. Alcohol poisoning will usually cause violent vomiting followed by extreme sleepiness, which then leads to passing out and even difficulty breathing. The end result of alcohol poisoning may be seizures or even death. A blackout should be a big warning sign that you're consuming way too much alcohol and may need help.

What if you were drugged? How can you know for sure? Waking up without your underwear and without any memory of the night before is really frightening because you have no idea whether you were raped, or even if you were raped by several guys. The implications of that are huge. If you believe you were slipped a date rape drug, there are tests that can detect the drugs, but they have to be done within hours. Reporting the event to the police is the best way to find out. They can direct you to health care where the tests can be done and you can get the medical and emotional attention you need.

"My friend was raped while she was drunk at a party. She won't tell anyone. How can I help her?"

The Full Scoop: Unfortunately, when many girls and women are raped, they don't tell anyone or report it to the police because they feel embarrassed or ashamed. No matter how a girl acts or dresses, nothing makes it okay for someone to rape her. Your friend probably feels partly to blame because she was drunk. In reality, your friend didn't have a choice in what happened to her, and she's just trying to survive the experience. What she does have a choice about is taking care of herself and getting medical attention so she can heal from it, both physically and emotionally.

You can help her understand that being drunk didn't give anyone the right to have sex with her. You can also help her understand the importance of getting medical attention and help with the emotional part of the healing. If your friend gets drunk frequently, this might be the event that gives her a reason to stop drinking. But if she doesn't get professional help in dealing with her trauma, she is at risk for depression, health problems, and drinking more. You can have a huge impact on her life if you can help her see the importance of reaching out for help.

"What are date rape drugs?"

Quickie Answer: The ones that get the most press include Rohypnol (rō HIP nall) and gamma hydroxybutyrate (GHB).

The Full Scoop: Rohypnol, better known as roofies, roach, forget-me pill, or the date rape drug, is a prescription medicine. It is an antianxiety medicine that is ten times more powerful than Valium. Some teens think it's safe because it's a prescription medication that comes in presealed bubble packs. Not safe at all. It's both a hypnotic and an amnestic. Hypnotic means you will do things you are told, as if you were hypnotized. Amnestic means you won't have any memory of what happened while you were under the influence of the drug. Scary. It takes effect as soon as thirty minutes after it's ingested and the effects can last up to eight hours.

Another date rape drug is known as "liquid ecstasy" or GHB, which stands for gamma hydroxybutyrate. It is popular as a date rape drug because it is a liquid that has no color, taste, or odor, and it can be slipped into a drink and not noticed. GHB causes hallucinations and intense highs but also causes rapid loss of consciousness and may even result in coma, especially when mixed with alcohol. **That's why you should never accept a drink that someone else has made for you.** If you have a drink at a party (alcoholic or not), make it yourself and keep it with you at all times.

"Are all date rapes related to alcohol or drugs?"

Quickie Answer: No, but most are.

The Full Scoop: The sad statistic is that one out of four girls will experience a sexual assault by the time they are twenty, and the most common time it happens is when a girl is under the influence of alcohol or drugs. Alcohol is by far the most common date rape drug. You may hear more about Rohypnol and GHB, but avoiding alcohol is the most important thing you can do to prevent date rape.

It's common to experiment with alcohol during high school and college, but if we can give you one piece of advice, it would be to avoid alcohol and drugs when you are around guys. It would be ideal to avoid alcohol altogether during your teen years. But if you choose to use it anyway, be very careful about where you are and whom you are with.

Here are some other strategies that may keep you from becoming a victim of alcohol-related date rape:

* Avoid alcohol and drug use.

* Don't accept a drink from anyone unless you watched it being made or opened. That includes nonalcoholic drinks. Date rape drugs can be colorless, odorless, and essentially undetectable in any flavored drink. Alcohol just increases the effect of date rape drugs.

* Keep your drink with you at all times.

* Beware of large vats of "punch" made with alcohol and fruity drinks. Fruit flavors can mask the taste of alcohol and you won't recognize how strong the drink is. Alcoholic "punches" at teen and college parties are usually very strong, which means very dangerous.

As a teen, sex is risky enough. If alcohol or drugs are added into the mix, the risks just aren't worth it. Don't let yourself lose control to alcohol. Too many bad things happen.

Think It Through

Part 1: The Party

•Key•
—— happened
----- could have happened

Tasha & Chelsea going out on Friday night

cute boys
alcohol
no parents
loud music
→ BIG PARTY

T & C find something else to do cuz they know this party has major potential for trouble.

Tasha & Chelsea go to the party

T & C get separated → ← Zach is out of town

Party gets busted by police

Tasha stays sober

Chelsea gets wasted

arrests for underage drinking

parents are notified

to be continued...

to be continued...

school officials find out

basketball players are suspended from team

some kids' parents think it's no big deal as long as they weren't driving

some kids get in huge trouble

Think It Through

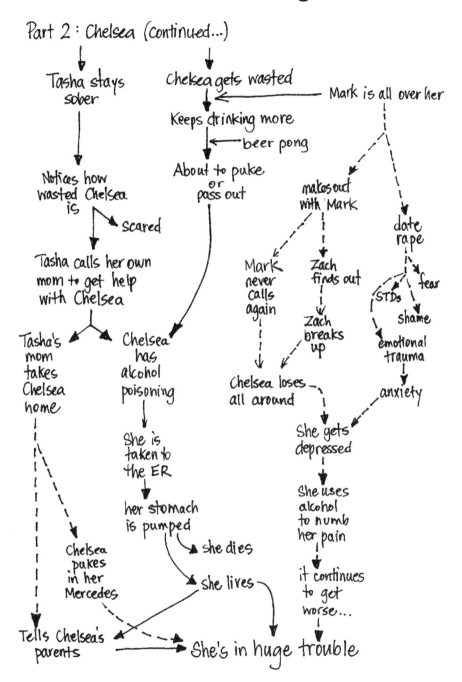

Part 2: Chelsea (continued...)

Tasha stays sober

Chelsea gets wasted ← Mark is all over her

Keeps drinking more

← beer pong

Notices how wasted Chelsea is

→ Scared

About to puke or pass out

makes out with Mark

date rape

Tasha calls her own mom to get help with Chelsea

Mark never calls again

Zach finds out

STDs → fear

shame

Tasha's mom takes Chelsea home

Chelsea has alcohol poisoning

Zach breaks up

emotional trauma

anxiety

Chelsea loses all around

She gets depressed

She is taken to the ER

Chelsea pukes in her Mercedes

She uses alcohol to numb her pain

her stomach is pumped

she dies

she lives

it continues to get worse...

Tells Chelsea's parents

She's in huge trouble

Think It Through

Part 3: Tasha (continued...)

Tasha drinks

Tasha stays sober

she's no help to anyone

helps Chelsea

Ty has been drinking a lot

Invites Tasha to leave with him

realizes Ty shouldn't drive

doesn't realize Ty is wasted

Takes his keys

he gets a ride home

doesn't take his keys

she leaves with him

he leaves without her & before she takes his keys

Coach finds out & Ty is kicked off team

he drives himself & some friends

Ty is in a car wreck

he walks away with no injuries & continues to drink

he is injured

he is killed.

he kills someone else

he gets away with it

this time

he is emotionally wrecked

his grades drop

loses option for college sports scholarship

next time may be different

performance is poor

alcohol becomes a "crutch"

Ty becomes an alcoholic ...

Chapter

"What's the best birth control method for teens?"

Staying pregnancy-free

A Real-Life Dilemma

There was nothing between Tasha and her Friday night flick except a down comforter, a bowl of buttered popcorn, and the remote. She smiled, snuggling under the covers. It had been a long week. She'd led the girls' basketball team to the county play-offs, made it through two midterms, and aced a chem lab that had disaster written all over it—making her mother, the doctor, very happy. She'd earned this. Tomorrow she was hanging with the girls: mall, manicures, and mingling with a few guys from school—maybe Ty Johnson if she got lucky. "Mmm, Ty . . ." she sighed, smiling. But tonight Tasha was into solitude. Besides, nobody else was willing to watch back-to-back-to-back chick flicks.

She'd just hit play when her cell phone rang, Justin Timberlakes's voice echoing through her bedroom. "Ah, if only . . ." she giggled, reaching for the phone and hitting the mute button. "This better be good. I'm on a twelve-hour vacation from life."

"Tasha? It's Reanne . . . Reanne Holliston."

"Reanne?" Chelsea, Amanda, or Sydney after ten, but she hardly talked to Reanne at school and never on the phone. "Um, what's up?"

"Sorry, I know it's kind of late, but I need your help. Actually, I need your mom's help."

Tasha nodded; she'd gotten two or three panic calls before. Lots of kids knew her mother ran the hospital emergency room. They'd want to know if Dr. Hart could get them birth control pills—without telling their parents—or what to do about some heinous itch they felt sure was fatal. Reanne had a pretty bad rep, so she could only imagine what this was all about. "What's wrong, Reanne?"

"Well, I'm kinda parked outside your house. Can I come in?"

"You're here? Now?"

"Um, yeah, it's . . . it's an emergency. It really can't wait."

Tasha's first reaction was to tell Reanne that if it was that much of an emergency, maybe she should hang up and dial 911—for God's sake, they weren't running a free clinic out of their kitchen. But her mother had always encouraged her to be helpful in situations like this, to be glad it wasn't her. "Okay, Reanne. Come to the back door. I'll be right down."

Tasha glanced around the dimly lit room, the warm bed, soggy popcorn, and a movie that most definitely shouldn't be watched on mute. She flipped it off and threw back the covers.

• • •

Ten minutes later Reanne Holliston was sitting at the Hart's kitchen table, Tasha on one side, her mother, in her bathrobe, on the other. Reanne had insisted that Tasha stay. Wonderful.

"You . . . you have to help me, Dr. Hart," she gulped, reaching for another tissue. "I can't believe it broke. I didn't think they could break . . . I never had one break before. Chad said he's never had one break before."

"They're latex, Reanne," Tasha said, rolling her eyes. "You've never seen a balloon pop? Same theory."

"Tasha! If you don't have anything helpful to add, you can leave the room," her mother said. "A broken condom is not a joke."

"Sorry," she mumbled, sitting back in her chair. "When did you and Chad Meyers hook up anyway? I didn't know you two were . . . together."

Reanne shrugged, biting a thumbnail. "About a week ago. I guess it, um, moved kind of fast. Usually I date a guy at least four times before I even consider sleeping with him . . . It's like a rule," she said, as if it deserved approval.

Tasha and her mother exchanged a knowing glance, but didn't say anything. She knew her mother wouldn't approve of Reanne's behavior. However, that would never stop her from helping a girl like Reanne—especially a girl like Reanne.

"So this just happened tonight?" Dr. Hart asked.

"Uh huh . . . at first, I didn't think too much about it. Then, well, pregnancy kind of runs in my family, so I thought maybe I ought to be worried."

"Runs in your family?" Dr. Hart's brow furrowed, looking curiously at her.

"Yeah, my sister got pregnant in high school, and so did my mom, so I figured I'd be a little smarter than they were."

"I see. Well, you were smart to do something about it tonight, that's for sure. How old are you, Reanne?"

"Sixteen," she said, wiping streaks of black mascara from her face.

"Well, then, I imagine you'll want to use emergency contraception. Do you already have a prescription? Do you have a doctor you can call for one?"

Reanne stared blankly.

Hesitantly, Dr. Hart added, "Okay. Well . . . you're in luck because I suppose I can give you a prescription. But it's not usually this easy to come by. Are you familiar with what it is?"

"No . . . I was hoping you could help me with all this."

"Emergency contraception is really just two birth control pills that you can take to help prevent pregnancy, like the name says, in an emergency."

Reanne's face brightened. "Oh my God, that's great, Dr. Hart. I'd heard there was something you could take, a pill. But I wasn't sure. Like, it's hard to know what's for real and what's just a rumor."

"If you were eighteen, you could buy it over the counter, but you'll need the prescription since you're younger. It's safer than aspirin, and it only contains the hormone progesterone, so it won't make you so sick. How it works is complicated, but basically it delays ovulation so you won't get pregnant. It's best to take it within seventy-two hours of having unprotected sex, but the sooner you take it, the better it works." The girl nodded, a smile starting to curve across her mouth. "Reanne, it will probably keep you from getting pregnant—this time—but it won't protect you from STDs. So I'm going to give you the prescription on one condition."

"What's that? Oh, please don't tell my mom. If she finds out she'll kill me."

Tasha leaned back in her chair, nodding. She knew what her mother was going to say next.

"I want you to come by the free family planning clinic. It's right across from the emergency room. If you're sexually active you need to be seen by a doctor, tested for STDs, and come up with a better plan for how you might avoid situations like this in the future."

"Sure, Dr. Hart, no problem. Whatever you want," Reanne said, her fingers inching toward the prescription Tasha's mother was writing.

But Tasha also knew what that meant. It made her angry, girls who were so careless, willing to risk their health, never mind their reputations. She also didn't like the idea of Reanne taking advantage of her mother's good intentions. She leaned back into the conversation, her hand slapping across the prescription. "You need to do it, Reanne. This is serious."

"I . . . I will, Tasha. Um, next week is kinda busy, but I'll get there. I swear."

"Sure you will."

"No, really, I will. It's just that . . . well, I've never been to that kind of doctor before . . ." Reanne bit her lip, staring at the prescription. "But I probably need to. I guess I'm kind of afraid what they'll tell me." Her voice softened, wavering a little. "You know, it's not like this at my house. I mean, I'd never be sitting at my kitchen table having a conversation like this with my mom."

"Is that right?" Dr. Hart said, raising an eyebrow at her own daughter. "You know what, Reanne? I bet Tasha would go with you to the clinic. In fact, I know she'd be happy to."

Tasha's mouth dropped open, as her mother gave the prescription to Reanne. "You follow the directions on the package. And I'll see you both Monday, at the clinic."

Doc Talk:
The Way **We See It**

DO YOU WORRY THAT GETTING ON SOME FORM of birth control makes sex seem way too planned? Does it make you feel better to believe that sex "just happens" because you get carried away in a flurry of romance? That it's not really a pre-meditated kind of thing? It may be like that on TV, but you're not on TV, remember? If you answered yes to any of the questions above, then it's time to climb out of fantasyland and into the real world where sex has consequences.

Planning ahead is a GOOD thing, especially when it comes to sex. So if you have had sex or if you are thinking about getting physical with your guy, you need to *think it through*. Consider all the possibilities and options. Ask yourself, "What is the best way for me to avoid pregnancy? How will I get my birth control? What will I do if I get pregnant? Am I sure I'm ready to have sex?" You have to face the fact that if you have sex, you are treading into the world of adult decisions, and you need to be mature and responsible about it all. You need to know what's available, what does and doesn't work, and make some decisions about how you expect to handle your health and the possible consequences. Yep. It's a big deal.

Taking care of yourself is important. You probably hope to get a good education, have a great job, and provide cool stuff and a happy home for a family one day. Protecting yourself against pregnancy *now* will help you do all these other things later. But you know what scares us? Most girls don't even try to get birth control until about six to twelve months *after* they've started having sex. Hello? For some, that's six months too late and three months before the baby is due. **Birth control matters. It allows you to have a baby when you are ready, not because "it just happened."** Doesn't a child deserve more than that from you? If you don't feel ready to manage birth control and use it correctly, you're not ready to have sex. Period.

We can always hope that teens will suddenly stop having sex and people will only have one sexual partner in their lifetime. There's nothing wrong with wishing. But in the meantime, and in the real world, we'll keep helping teens understand the facts about sex, health, and birth control. We'll keep working to get teens (and adults!) who decide to have sex to protect themselves against unwanted pregnancy and sexually transmitted infections. So, learn all you can, think it through, and plan ahead.

This chapter should provide some of the information you need to know about birth control and preventing pregnancy. We won't go into the nitty-gritty details about each method, but consider it an overview. We don't expect to answer everything, and we certainly can't take the place of a good conversation with your doctor or a knowledgeable parent. If you need birth control, find out all you can about using your method correctly. So keep learning, keep asking questions, and remember, you can always e-mail us more questions and look for the answers on our website. Meanwhile, we'll give you the truth and the lies, the ups and the downs, and the full scoop on birth control.

YOU Asked! "How does birth control work?"

A Long Quickie Answer: Birth control (aka contraception) works in one of three ways: (1) it stops ovulation; (2) it kills the sperm; or (3) it creates a barrier between the egg and the sperm.

The Full Scoop: There are three major types of birth control. And really, there are four when you include abstinence, which is clearly the most effective! Besides abstinence, there are hormonal methods (the pill, patch, rings, and implants), barrier methods (condoms, spermicides, sponge, diaphragm), and permanent methods (getting "tubes tied" in a woman or a vasectomy for men).

Hormonal contraceptives are the most commonly used birth control among young women. The "hormones" in birth control are forms of estrogen and progesterone. All hormonal contraceptives contain progesterone and some contain both estrogen and progesterone. The estrogen works to prevent the ovary from creating the cyst that the egg matures in each month. No cyst, no mature egg to ovulate. The progesterone works primarily by preventing ovulation, but it also thickens the mucus in the cervix so sperm have a hard time getting through, and it thins the lining of the endometrium so it's not fluffy enough for implantation to occur.

If you think about the ways that hormonal birth control methods work, you'll understand why they also make periods lighter (thinner endometrium) and more predictable (the hormones take over your natural hormonal cycles), and why they practically eliminate period cramps (lighter flow means less cramps). If they contain estrogen and progesterone, they also decrease problems related to ovarian cysts and reduce the risk of getting ovarian cancer.

"Which birth control is best for teen girls?"

Another Long Quickie: Abstinence is the best method for preventing pregnancy. For teens who choose to have sex, a "belt and suspenders" or double-your-safety approach is best. That means you rely on two methods: a barrier method for STD prevention and a hormonal method for more reliable pregnancy prevention.

A Very Large Scoop: Can you remember to take a pill every day, or is it easier to change a patch once a week? Is it better to see your doctor and have four shots a year, or can you place a soft silicone ring in your vagina once a month? It is a personal choice. If you choose the method that seems most comfortable for you, and you use it exactly when and how you are supposed to, you can expect your birth control to be 98–99 percent effective. That's the "perfect use" effectiveness. But **the "real-life" effectiveness is always lower, like 85–95 percent because of human error. Sometimes that extra effectiveness is really up to you and how carefully you use your method.**

Now let's talk about all the different types of hormonal contraception. Understanding how each method is used, its side effects, and the benefits of using it can help you make a more informed decision. Benefits? Absolutely. Besides protecting you against an unwanted pregnancy, many hormonal methods of birth control have helpful side effects.

The Pill

If you can remember to take a pill every day around the same time, then the pill may be your first choice. Once you get into the habit, it becomes much easier, but establishing a new habit takes an average of about three months, so be careful! To make it easier to remember, some girls set an alarm on their cell phone, tape their pills to their bathroom mirror, or put them by their toothbrush where they see them every morning. For girls who are already taking medication daily and have no trouble remembering to take them, using "the pill" can be very easy.

Birth control pills come in lots of different strengths and schedules, but basically, the standard pills come in packs of twenty-eight pills (four weeks' worth). They provide estrogen and progesterone for about three to three and a half weeks, then they have "placebo" pills for the last three to seven days. When the hormones stop (and you are on your placebo pills), your period will start. As soon as you finish the last pill in one pack, you need to start the first pill in a new pack on the following day. Starting the new pack helps stop your period and makes sure you don't go too long without the hormones (since the hormones are what prevent pregnancy). If you are even one day late starting a new pack, it increases the risk for pregnancy in the next cycle.

If you take the pill every day at the same time and never ever miss a pill, it will be 98–99 percent effective. But guess what? We're all human and sometimes we forget; sometimes we get off schedule. **Like to sleep in late on the weekends? Forget to pick up your next pack from the pharmacy? Go to your friend's house for the night? Those kinds of things can make the pill fail.** Honestly, studies have shown that teen girls on the pill miss an average of two to three pills a month. That's not the recommended way to take them, but that's reality, and it reduces the effectiveness. Missing three pills a month can reduce the effectiveness to no better than condoms. It's one more reason for the belt-and-suspenders approach.

The pill is convenient and pretty reliable, but it has side effects like nausea, breast tenderness, headaches, moodiness, and irregular spotting. The good news is that most of these side effects go away after three or four months on the pill. If they are severe or not getting any better, then you may need to try a different pill. There are over eighty (eighty!) different birth control pills out there, all with slightly different doses or slightly different forms of the hormones, so obviously there's not one that works for everyone. Sometimes it takes trying two or three different pills before you find one that works best for you.

The benefits to taking the pill include the following:

• Makes periods much more predictable • Decreases the amount of menstrual blood flow (usually by at least half of what you normally have) • Improves menstrual cramps • Improves acne • Helps prevent iron-deficiency anemia • Helps prevent ovarian cysts • Reduces the symptoms of premenstrual syndrome (or PMS, which includes moodiness before your period) • Helps prevent breast cysts and fibrocystic breast problems • Reduces the risk of ovarian cancer and endometrial cancer • Decreases the chances of getting pelvic inflammatory disease • Decreases the risk of tubal pregnancy

The Patch

The patch looks like a large, square Band-Aid, and it works by slowly releasing estrogen and progesterone through your skin into your bloodstream. Nothing to swallow. You change your patch once a week for three weeks, then you go one week without a patch. The patchless week is when you'll get your period. It is exactly as effective as the pill, and you only have to remember to change it three times a month, so **the patch may actually be more effective for girls who have trouble remembering their pill every day.**

The side effects of the patch are the same as the pill, plus the sticky issues from the glue that holds it onto your skin. Like with Band-Aids, you can get skin irritation and also that "dirty-looking ring" around the edges. Oh well. At least you can stick it in places that don't usually show. Talk about sticky. The patch has great sticking power, even when you are swimming, sweating, or sitting in a sauna.

The patch puts more estrogen into the bloodstream than the pill or the ring. Whether that increases the risk for problems is not clear yet, but most women do fine with it. The other concern with the patch is that it may not work as well as other hormonal methods for girls who weigh more than about 200 pounds. As far as benefits, the patch should have the same benefits as the pill because it works the same way.

The Vaginal Ring

This is a soft, flexible, thin ring of silicone that you place in your vagina once a month. Really. You leave it in your vagina for three weeks, then remove it for the fourth week to have your period. It can stay in during sex, during running, during whatever. If it slips out (and it does less than 2 percent of the time), you have three hours to get it back in before you mess up the hormone levels and lose its effectiveness. Speaking of effective, it ranks high at 98 percent effective when used correctly. And it's **easy to use it correctly because you only have to remember something once a month—well, really twice: take it out after three weeks and put a new one in a week later.**

One of the more appealing things about the ring is the low rate of side effects. It has the lowest amount of hormones of all of the hormonal contraceptives, and the hormones get into your bloodstream through the walls of the vagina. Like with the patch, that means there is nothing to swallow, so nausea is not really an issue. It also should carry the same benefits as the pill and the patch, but with fewer side effects.

For some girls, the ring is not an option because they don't feel comfortable sticking it in and taking it out. Hint: you have to use your fingers. To that, we say, get real. If you are having sex, you should certainly feel okay about your own finger going in your vagina, especially if it's for birth control purposes. But we understand that some will just never be okay with that. That's why there are lots of options out there.

The other major hormonal types of contraception are shots (such as Depo-Provera, or DMPA) and implants. We have another question devoted to that, so read on.

The biggest problem with hormonal types of birth control is that **they DO NOT protect you against sexually transmitted infections.** You should know that by now, but there's more on STD prevention in Chapter 8.

"Is there anyone who shouldn't take the pill?"

The Full Scoop: There are some conditions that absolutely make the pill too dangerous, but most of these conditions only affect adults. It would be rare for a teen to have any concerns.

For teens, there are other things that need to be checked carefully by your doctor before you use the pill, patch, or ring, because for some girls, the pill might worsen the problem or cover up what is really wrong. These things include the following:

* if you've stopped having your period and it's not clear why

* if you are a heavy cigarette smoker (that means more than five cigarettes a day)

* if you have depression, especially if it has been difficult to control

* if you have migraine headaches that cause numbness, tingling, temporary weakness, or temporary blindness

* if you have irregular spotting

Another thing to keep in mind is that there are some medications that can make the pill/patch/ring less effective. Some uncommon antibiotics and most of the medications used to prevent seizures in girls with epilepsy will interfere with the effectiveness of your birth control. Most of the antibiotics used to treat acne, respiratory infections, strep throat, and other common infections will not interfere with birth control pills. But **if you are taking any other medications, it's always a good idea to check with your doctor or pharmacist to make sure your other meds won't mess up your pills and vice versa.**

"How do you know which pill to use?"

Quickie Answer: You don't have to. Let your doctor make that decision.

The Full Scoop: The pill with the sexiest ads isn't always the brand that's best for you. With so many types of pills available, how's a girl to know which one is best for her? That's what your doctor is for.

Fortunately, most girls will do fine on most of the available pills. But sometimes, the side effects become so bothersome that you need to switch to a different one. If you've given your body enough time to adjust to your pills, and you're taking them correctly, most side effects will disappear on their own after the first three months. If you just can't handle the side effects at all, or it's been longer than three months and they are no better, then you will want to try another pill.

Your doctor will need to know about your side effects to help you choose a pill that will reduce the symptoms you are experiencing.

What you DON'T want to do is stop your pills without talking to your doctor. **As annoying as the side effects can be, a pregnancy would be worse.** Make sure you don't stop any birth control without speaking to your doctor first to make sure you stay protected until you can switch the dose or the method.

"What happens if I miss a pill?"

Quickie Answer: **You increase your risk for pregnancy.**

The Full Scoop: You're only human and things happen that interrupt your usual routine. But don't let that make you think that it's no big deal to miss a pill. Missed pills are the reason why the pill is only 92 percent effective in real life. If you never miss a pill and take them around the same time every day, it can be 99 percent effective. Every pill you miss increases your risk for pregnancy. **That's another reason we always recommend that double-your-confidence, belt-and-suspenders, pad-and-tampon, breath-mint-and-gum, hormonal contraception-AND-condom approach to protecting yourself.**

If you are on the pill, the package will come with detailed instructions on how to take them and what to do if you miss one, two, or more. Basically, you'll take the missed pill as soon as you realize you missed it, or as soon as you can get to it. But it can get complicated if you've missed more than one pill. If you're ever in doubt, call your doctor's office or clinic and ask. Don't just stop them altogether because you can't figure it out!

If you are on the pill, it's also important to know about emergency contraception (EC). If you miss pills, emergency contraception can help prevent pregnancy even after you've had sex. There's more on EC later.

The other thing to realize is that missing pills will often cause some vaginal spotting or bleeding. How much you bleed may depend on the dose you are taking and where in the pack you are. Most of the time, the bleeding stops once you are back to taking the pills every day again.

"Will birth control pills make me gain weight?"

Quickie Answer: **Nope.**

The Full Scoop: Birth control pills got a reputation for causing weight gain back in the days when they had higher doses of hormones. The newer low-dose pills that are usually prescribed for teens today do not cause weight gain. There's research to prove it. What really happens is that teenagers are still developing a more adult body, which means there's a normal amount of weight gain going on anyway. The other issue is that many teens start eating more fast food when they can drive; they don't have mandatory PE as often; and they get less exercise than when they were younger. So as a teen, it becomes more important to **pay attention to the food you eat and your activity level because those are the things that determine whether you gain weight, not the pill.**

"Will birth control pills help with my acne?"

Quickie Answer: YES!!!!

The Full Scoop: The pill is actually approved and recommended as a medical treatment for acne. Girls on the pill will notice a significant improvement in their acne after three to four months. If you've tried topical medications or antibiotics and still have problems, the pill might be the solution for you. Talk with your doctor about it. You don't have to be sexually active or need the pill to help period problems. Just having acne is enough of a reason to be put on it. And it really does help.

"Are there other medical reasons to take birth control?"

The Full Scoop: Just like with acne, there are other medical conditions that will improve with certain birth control methods. If you have irregular periods, painful periods, very heavy periods, anemia, polycystic ovarian syndrome, epilepsy, sickle cell disease, or breast pain, talk with your doctor about whether contraceptives are a good option for you.

"Do birth control pills cause cancer?"

The Full Scoop: Let's give you the great news first. Birth control pills actually protect girls and women against uterine cancer (cancer of the uterus) and ovarian cancer (you got it . . . cancer of the ovary). If you take birth control pills, even for one year, your risk for endometrial cancer is cut in half, and that protection lasts at least fifteen years beyond when you stop the pill. Similarly, the longer a female uses oral contraceptive pills, the lower her risk for ovarian cancer. That's huge! If you have any family history of either of these cancers, taking OCs would be important for prevention purposes. **Even if you don't have these cancers in your family, you will still benefit from the protection.**

And there's more good news. Breast cancer has been the biggest concern for many girls and women who use any type of hormones. For several decades, scientists from all over the world have studied hormonal birth control and breast cancer, and they've found no clear link. The most recent and important studies have provided reassurance. The largest study showed that using the pill did not increase the risk of breast cancer, even for those women who used it as a teen, used higher doses, and had a family history of breast cancer. There may be an exception that applies to women who carry the genetic mutation that puts them at particularly high risk for breast cancer. We need more research on this group. In general, though, **the pill has not been shown to increase the risk of breast cancer.**

"If I take birth control in my teens, will it be harder to have a baby later?"

The Full Scoop: It's another myth. Taking birth control won't do anything to harm your ability to get pregnant in the future. In fact, research shows that girls on the pill don't get pelvic inflammatory disease (PID) as often as girls who are not on the pill (we discuss this in detail in Chapter 8). That's not saying that the pill prevents STDs, but it does mean that if you get gonorrhea or chlamydia while you are on the pill, it is less likely that the infection will move up into your uterus and cause PID. And since PID is the number one cause of infertility in the United States, the pill can be seen as something that may protect you from that problem.

Another concern has to do with the hormones affecting your fertility. After you stop the pill, your natural hormones will return to normal quickly. You'll usually get your period "naturally" by the next month, but within a few months at the most. So the hormones in the pill won't interfere with your body's natural hormones and ability to get pregnant after you stop taking it.

"What is the birth control shot?"

Quickie Answer: **Depo-Provera, aka DMPA.**

The Full Scoop: The shot is called depot medroxyprogesterone acetate. Since that's such a mouthful, we call it Depo-Provera or just DMPA. It's hormonal birth control that contains only progesterone. No estrogen. It works by preventing ovulation, thickening the mucus in the cervix, and thinning out the endometrium so the embryo can't implant.

The most appealing thing about DMPA is that the shot lasts three months, so you only have to think about it four times a year. For girls who have trouble remembering to take a pill, change their patch, or put a ring in their vagina, this can be a lifesaver. It is more than 99 percent effective as long as you get the shots within two weeks of when they are due.

Sound too good to be true? Well, there are some negatives:

* Irregular spotting is common, especially in the first three to six months. After a year of being on it, most girls don't have periods anymore—and that's okay in this case.

* DMPA can increase your appetite, so some girls will experience weight gain on it. If you have a hard time controlling your appetite or eating healthy when you are hungry, DMPA may not be for you.

* A small percentage of girls feel moody or depressed on it.

* After stopping DMPA, it may take six months to a year for your periods to come back or return to normal. Even if your periods haven't come back yet, you can still get pregnant, so if you're having sex, protect yourself with another method!

* Girls on DMPA may experience a decrease in their bone density. Some doctors worry about girls staying on DMPA for more than a couple of years. Bone density is important for lifetime bone strength and to prevent fractures or breaks.

"Can I rinse the sperm out of my vagina to help prevent pregnancy?"

Quickie Answer: No! That's called a douche, and it's definitely NOT recommended!

The Full Scoop: We've heard lots of crazy stories of things girls and women do right after sex to prevent pregnancy . . . like shaking up a soda and letting it squirt into the vagina, jumping up and down to get the sperm out, or sniffing pepper to make themselves sneeze. Add the douching-to-prevent-pregnancy thing to your list of big, fat myths. Hello? Aren't we all smarter than that by now?

You can shake, jump, sneeze, rinse, and squirt all you want, but none of it will help. In fact, if you douche after sex, it can be dangerous, because it will increase your risk for a tubal pregnancy and for pelvic inflammatory disease. Douching can also disturb the normal bacteria in the vagina and make you more at risk for bacterial vaginosis. So no douches, please.

If sperm have already made it into your vagina and aren't blocked by something (condom, sponge, diaphragm . . . keep reading, we'll talk about all of them), the only way to prevent pregnancy at that point is to take emergency contraception (EC).

"Can you get pregnant if you have sex during your period?"

Quickie Answer: Yep.

The Full Scoop: You can definitely get pregnant if you have sex during your period. For one thing, sperm can live up to seven days, so even if you are having your period and ovulate a week later, it's possible that one of those guys is still hanging around.

Also, as we said before, teen girls usually have no clue when they ovulate. Things such as stress, exercise, medications, and just hormonal changes can cause a girl to ovulate early or late. You can never be too sure. Birth control and protection against STDs are always critical if you are having sex, whether you are on your period or not.

Myth Bust!

You can't get pregant if . . .

While we're on the subject of myths, here's another list for you. **Call this your big, fat myth list and don't believe anything on it!** You can't get pregnant if . . .

- It's your first time to have sex
- You are having sex during your period
- Your guy pulls out before he ejaculates
- He doesn't put his penis all the way in
- You have sex in a pool, hot tub, shower, or bath. Hot water will not kill sperm or make them float out of you.
- You don't have an orgasm
- You jump up and down after sex
- You make yourself sneeze after sex
- You stay on top during sex
- You squirt a soda or other fluid in the vagina after sex

These are all FALSE, FALSE, FALSE!!!

"What is emergency contraception?"

Quickie Answer: It's birth control pills that can help prevent pregnancy AFTER unprotected sex—which is an emergency! It is not an abortion pill, so it will not work if you are already pregnant.

The Full Scoop: Emergency contraception (EC) is not a substitute for reliable birth control, but think of it as a last-ditch backup plan. The only EC marketed in the United States is called Plan B®. It is available without a prescription if you are over eighteen years old (and yes, guys can buy it too). It's kept behind the pharmacy counter, so you have to ask for it. If you're under eighteen, you'll need a prescription to get it. Plan B contains two pills that contain progesterone. No estrogen. That means it has few side effects, and it's safer than taking aspirin.

The sooner you take it after unprotected sex, the better it prevents pregnancy. The packaging on Plan B says you take the first pill within seventy-two hours (that's three days for you math haters) and take the second pill twelve hours later. More recent studies have shown that Plan B works just as well if you take both pills at the same time. And it still works (just not as well) up to five days after the emergency moment rather than just three days.

Because of the importance of taking it ASAP, it's a great idea to ask your doctor for a prescription for it BEFORE you really need it. You never know when you might end up with a broken condom or when you might miss a couple of pills. If you're lucky and very careful, you may never need it. But if you do, you'll be relieved you can take it quickly. That's called planning ahead and playing it smart.

If your doctor won't prescribe it, you can contact your local health clinic or Planned Parenthood clinic (1-800-230-PLAN). If you have trouble getting a prescription or don't know where to look, you can also call 1-888-NOT2LATE (1-888-668-2528) to find doctors in your area who will prescribe it. To learn more about it, look online at www.go2planB.com.

You may have also heard that you can take regular birth control pills as EC. It's true, but it can be confusing. Also, since regular birth control pills have estrogen as well as progesterone, there may be more side effects, particularly nausea and vomiting. There are eighteen brands of pills that are approved by the FDA for use as EC pills. Ask your doctor if you are on one of them. If so, find out how to use it as EC. Each brand has different directions, so make sure you get it right by talking with a professional.

After taking EC, it's also important to make sure you take the steps to prevent needing it again. **Remember—it's for emergencies.** You shouldn't try to use it as regular birth control. If you weren't on any birth control at all, get some! If your emergency was a broken condom, make sure you know how to use them properly. If it's because you missed too many pills in your normal pack, do something to help you remember them, like setting the alarm on your cell phone, taping them to your mirror, or keeping them with your toothbrush. Link them with something you do every morning or every night so you don't have any more emergencies like this!

"Does emergency contraception cause abortions?"

Quickie Answer: **Definitely not.**

The Full Scoop: Sometimes people get EC confused with the abortion pill, RU-486. They are totally different. EC is just progesterone, and it works just like regular birth control pills to prevent ovulation, thicken the mucus in the cervix, and change the endometrium so a pregnancy can't implant and grow there.

If you are already pregnant, EC won't do anything to the pregnancy. In fact, progesterone is the hormone actually given to some pregnant women (who have had complications before) to help prevent miscarriages. So, it definitely doesn't cause abortions, and it doesn't cause any birth defects or pregnancy complications. EC is a great way to PREVENT unwanted pregnancies and abortions.

"What exactly is an abortion?"

The Full Scoop: There are different types of abortion. Some happen naturally, and that is called a miscarriage or spontaneous abortion. For a variety of reasons, about half of all pregnancies miscarry. Most of them happen very early in the pregnancy, sometimes before the woman even knows she's pregnant.

The type of abortion that most people think of when they hear that word is an induced abortion. This can be done either with medication or through a surgical procedure.

A medical abortion is done with prescription pills that are only available under the care of a physician. Usually, this type of abortion is only recommended if the pregnancy is less than seven weeks along. One pill is given to end the pregnancy. A couple of days later, another medication is given to make the uterus contract and expel the pregnancy. This usually causes cramping and bleeding that may last up to a couple of weeks. Medical abortions are successful 92–95 percent of the time when the medications are used as directed. After a medical abortion, an ultrasound is important to make sure the procedure worked. If it doesn't work, a surgical abortion is recommended.

Surgical abortions are done in an office or operating room and may or may not involve anesthesia. The doctor stretches the opening of the cervix and uses a suction device and a scraping device to remove the pregnancy from the uterus. A surgical abortion is over faster than a medical abortion, but it requires surgery. If a pregnancy is more than three or four months along, abortion becomes more dangerous because the fetus is larger and there is usually more bleeding. Most states allow abortions through the fourth month, but each state has different regulations and laws about abortion services.

"Can I get an abortion without my parents finding out?

Quickie Answer: Probably not, unless you are seventeen or eighteen. It depends on your state's laws.

The Full Scoop: The laws governing abortion vary from state to state, so the **regulations and restrictions will depend on where you live.**

Most states have specific laws that address parental notice or permission for minors seeking an abortion. That's probably because lawmakers would like to see a perfect world where abortion is recognized as a big deal and girls facing such a big decision would benefit from their parents' support. Unfortunately, some parents won't offer the support that girls need but will try to dictate her decision instead. For most girls, facing a teen pregnancy is overwhelming. If you are faced with this decision, whether you decide to abort or continue the pregnancy, the support of an adult who loves you can be the most helpful thing in the world. This decision is huge and has long-term implications. Knowing your parents are on your side and support you even in difficult times can help you cope with your decision, plan for the future, and avoid regret.

"If I've been dating the same guy for a long time and I'm on birth control pills, do I really need to use condoms, too?"

Quickie Answer: Absolutely! For pregnancy prevention and STD protection.

The Full Scoop: Since most girls miss a pill here and there, it's smart to use a backup method all the time. Besides, the pill and other hormonal birth control methods do nothing, nada, zilch to protect you against STDs. We hear girls explain how important STD protection is with hook-ups (casual sex—which we don't recommend), but that in a monogamous relationship (sex with only each other), condoms aren't as important. What's up with that? **Don't you care enough about yourself and your BF to make sure you are both protected against STDs?** Many of the most serious STDs have no symptoms or don't cause any symptoms for months after someone is infected. So unless you've never had sex and neither has he—meaning you are both each other's first sexual partners—you can never know for sure if there's an STD hiding in one of you. The only way to know you're not passing along or getting an STD is by not having sex. The next best way to protect you and your BF is to use a condom correctly and consistently every time you have sex.

"Is it possible to get pregnant if semen gets on you but not during intercourse?"

Quickie Answer: Only if it ends up close to your vagina.

The Full Scoop: Maybe you're messing around, no clothes on, but not really having sex in the penis-in-vagina sense of the word. If he ejaculates and the semen gets near your vagina, there may be a few überdetermined sperm that will find their way in and make the trip all the way to the egg. Remember, there are millions of sperm, and it only takes one. It's not very likely, but it is possible.

"If a guy pulls out before he comes, will that work in an emergency (like when you don't have a condom)?"

Quickie Answer: Work for what? For him maybe. But not for protecting you against STDs or pregnancy. Don't consider the lack of a condom an emergency. Consider it an obstacle that will absolutely prevent you from having sex.

The Full Scoop: Pulling out as a method of birth control has been around since someone finally discovered sperm and linked it to the cause of pregnancy. **We call that method "pull and pray," or else we call it stupid.** There are several reasons why it's no good. First, you could still be exposed to STDs through the skin-to-skin contact and the pre-ejaculate fluid that escapes before he really ejaculates. You could also be exposed to sperm that way. Even though pre-ejaculate doesn't usually contain sperm, it sometimes does. That's not reliable enough. And the biggest reason not to rely on the "pull and pray" method is that many teen guys don't always know exactly when they are going to ejaculate and don't always have the tremendous self-control that it takes to pull out just when it's feeling so good for them. And that's when it has to happen. **If he's even a few seconds late, it's a sperm party in your vagina, and you've just had unprotected real sex.** That's scary and very risky.

Don't count on someone else (no matter how much you love and trust him) to handle all the birth control in your relationship. It's your body, and it will be your pregnancy. If you are having sex, you have to commit to taking care of yourself by using a reliable (preferably hormonal) method of birth control and insisting on condom use every time you have sex.

"How effective are condoms?"

Quickie Answer: About 86 percent in real life.

The Full Scoop: Condoms can be 98, even 99 percent effective in preventing pregnancy if used correctly *every single* *time* you have sex. That means out of 100 girls or women who are having sex and using condoms correctly and consistently, only 2 would get pregnant in a year. That's very effective, even though nobody wants to be one of the two who gets pregnant. In real life, however, the effectiveness is only 86 percent, meaning 14 out of 100 girls will get pregnant in a year of condom use. Why the difference? Because sometimes condoms aren't used correctly, sometimes teens get carried away and don't use a condom, and sometimes condoms break.

Knowing the right way to use a condom is not just something guys need to know. Again, it's YOUR body, so know how to protect it. Here's how to use them correctly. Using them consistently is up to you.

* Use a condom every single time you have sex. That includes vaginal, oral, and anal.

* Don't use your teeth or fingernails to open the condom package. They can rip.

* Don't unroll the condom until it is in position on the penis. Hint: it will only unroll in one direction. Make sure you know which side to unroll from.

* Never try to put a condom on a flaccid (soft) penis. It needs to be put on when the penis is erect and before the penis gets near the vagina. If the penis is not circumcised, pull the foreskin back before putting on the condom.

* Before unrolling the condom down the penis, hold on to about the last half-inch of it to leave some room where the semen will collect after ejaculation. If the condom has something called a reservoir tip, that space is already built in, but you still need to

make sure it doesn't flatten out on the head of the penis.

* If you use a gel or liquid as a lubricant, make sure it is "water-based." That means it doesn't contain any petroleum-based products like Vaseline, baby oil, or hand lotion. These substances will dissolve the latex in the condom and create holes.

* Make sure the penis is pulled out while it's still erect and that one of you is holding the bottom of the condom around the base of the penis to keep it from slipping off. If the penis becomes soft before he pulls out, semen can leak out of the base of the condom and you've lost your protection.

* Inspect the condom for any holes or breaks. If a condom breaks and you need emergency contraception (EC), get it!

* Don't use condoms that are expired (the date is on the box and on the packet, and they're usually good for about five years).

* Don't use a condom that has been in a wallet for a long time. Latex will tear more easily if it has been through big temperature changes, rough handling, or if it's just plain old. If a condom is damaged, discolored, or sticky, it's best to get a newer one.

"Can condoms rip or break easily?"

Quickie Answer: Most research shows that condoms only break about 2 percent of the time, and it's usually during intercourse or withdrawal.

"Can someone be allergic to condoms?"

The Full Scoop: Most condoms are made from latex, and the most effective condoms for STD prevention are latex. Latex allergies are not very common, but they occur more often among people who are exposed to it a lot, such as people who work in the health-care field where they have to wear latex gloves and people who have had a lot of surgeries (by surgeons wearing latex gloves). It might also be true of people who have had a lot of sex with a lot of latex condoms. The more you are exposed, the more your risk for developing an allergy.

Before we get into explaining latex allergy, we first have to reassure you that most vaginal burning or irritation that happens after sex is NOT a latex allergy. It is more likely to be from a spermicide (used as a lubricant on some condoms) or a vaginal infection. Vaginal burning, itching, and swelling are also the most common symptoms of a latex allergy. Either way, if you experience these symptoms after sex, you need to see a gynecologist or another physician who can evaluate your symptoms, make a diagnosis, and help you know whether you need to avoid latex or not.

For people who have a true latex allergy, there are condoms made from a plastic substance (called polyurethane) and others made from "lambskin" (but they're really made from animal intestines). Both of these types will protect against pregnancy, but the **lambskin condoms do NOT protect against STDs,** so they are not recommended for teens. The polyurethane condoms offer STD protection, but they slip off more often and break about three times more frequently than latex condoms. They're not perfect, but they're better than nothing.

"Are there condoms for women?"

Quickie Answer: Yes, there is one on the market, and it's called Reality®. Good name. In reality, girls who are having sex should always take responsibility for protecting themselves.

The Full Scoop: The Reality® female condom is made from polyurethane. It has two rings (one large, one medium) connected by a long flexible tube. One end is closed and one is open. The closed end goes into your vagina and the open end stays on the outside against your vulva. Reality comes with a non-spermicidal lubricant already in it.

By now, we're sure you know about double-your-safety protection, but this is one exception. Never use a male condom at the same time as a female condom. The friction will cause the male condom to come off or the female condom to move farther inside the vagina.

"What is spermicide?"

Quickie Answer: Spermicide is actually a detergent that kills sperm and some bacteria in the vagina. It is best used in combination with another contraceptive method.

The Full Scoop: Spermicides are cheap, easy to get without a prescription, and easy to use. But they should always be used in combination with a condom for adequate protection against STDs and pregnancy. There are lots of types to choose from: jelly, cream, foam, melting suppository, foaming tablet, and film. Whatever the form, it is placed in the vagina no longer than one hour before sex. If it's been longer than that, or if you're having sex again, you have to put in another "serving." Used alone, spermicide only offers about 75 percent protection against pregnancy. See why you need to use it with another birth control method?

Research has shown that spermicides can kill many of the bacteria and viruses that cause STDs, but it doesn't adequately kill HIV. And actually, it does a better job of killing bacteria in test tubes than it does in the human body where it really counts. There is even some research that indicates that **spermicides can increase the risk of getting HIV in women who have sex frequently.** That's because the chemicals that kill the sperm and bacteria can also damage the walls of the vagina. Damaged vaginal tissue provides places where the HIV can get into the bloodstream. So don't count on spermicide to offer you protection against STDs.

The most common problems with spermicide use include vaginal irritation or burning, which affect up to one in every twenty females who use it. Using spermicides also increases the risk for bladder infections and may increase the chances of getting a vaginal yeast infection.

"I saw the sponge in the condom aisle. What's that?"

Quickie Answer: A barrier type of birth control that also contains spermicide. It's literally a sponge that you place inside the vagina before having sex.

The Full Scoop: The contraceptive sponge is placed (using your fingers) deep in the vagina against the cervix. It works as a barrier to prevent sperm from getting through the cervix. Just in case some keep going, the sponge absorbs them and kills them with spermicide. It can be placed in the vagina right before sex or up to twenty-four hours before. The most important thing to know is that it should be left in for six hours after sex to make sure it has thoroughly absorbed and killed all the sperm. Oh, and **make sure you are still using a condom for STD protection if you are using the sponge to prevent pregnancy.**

"Do any teens use things like a diaphragm or the IUD?"

The Full Scoop: There are other contraceptive methods out there that teens don't typically use. The reasons they aren't popular for teens are usually related to the way they are used, the risk for infection, or the permanence of the method. Obviously teens don't get their tubes tied because that's permanent. The diaphragm is used by some teens, but most find it too awkward to put in and take out of their vagina. The IUD is a device that is inserted into the uterus and it's not recommended for anyone at risk for STDs. For most teens, the STD risk is too high, so doctors won't recommend it.

For some very mature teens, however, one of these methods may be appropriate—especially if they can't use a hormonal method. If you're in that category, you need to have a serious discussion with your doctor about these other methods to see if one might work well for you.

Think It Through

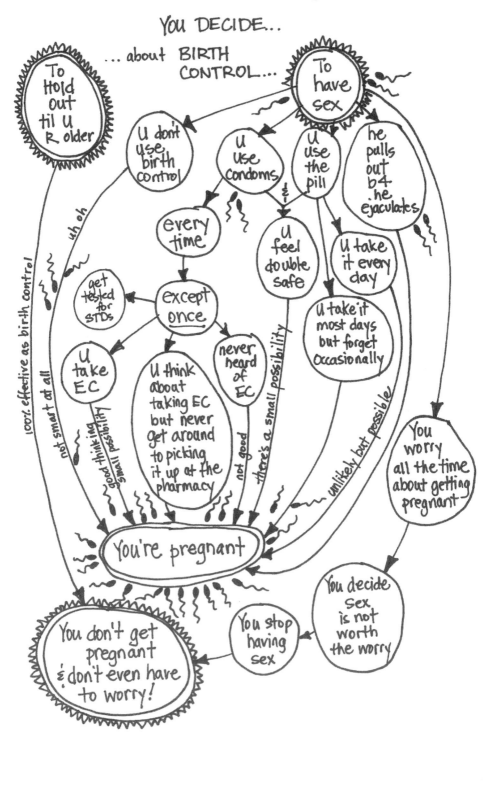

Think It Through

Reanne needs birth control

Tasha's mom is a doctor...and she seems pretty nice

Reanne needs STD testing <u>and</u> birth control

she provides EC this one time

she won't provide longer-term birth control cuz Reanne also needs STD testing and a doctor of her own

she asks her friends

one tells her about a free health clinic

Some say "don't worry! Just use a condom!"

Reanne talks with her own mom

her mom does not approve of her having sex but takes her to a doctor for healthcare

her mom tells her sex before marriage is wrong. Say no to sex and she won't need birth control

she asks her guidance counselor

she is referred to her county's health department and planned parenthood

She calls & makes an appointment

She is counseled about birth control options and STDs. She has a chance to ask questions and get straightforward answers. She realizes that having sex is a big responsibility. She is tested for STDs and knows she has an important decision to make about birth control. She needs something reliable and easy for her to use correctly..... She wants to know.....

Think It Through

"Exactly how reliable are these methods?"
like...

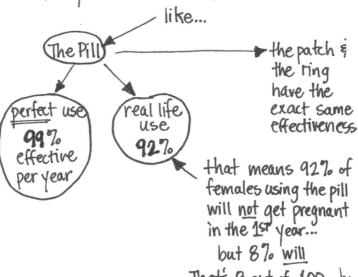

The Pill

perfect use
99%
effective
per year

real life
use
92%

the patch &
the ring
have the
exact same
effectiveness

that means 92% of
females using the pill
will <u>not</u> get pregnant
in the <u>1st</u> year...
but 8% <u>will</u>
That's 8 out of 100...hmmm...

"What about the other methods?"

and who's
perfect ?!

	<u>perfect use</u>	<u>real life use</u>
condoms ———————➤	98%	85%
depo Provera ——————➤	99+%	97%
sponge ———————➤	91%	84%
spermicide ——————➤	82%	71%
withdrawal ———————➤	no such thing	73%
Implanon ———————➤	99+%	99+%

"and if you use nothing?"
85% <u>will be pregnant</u> within a year...yikes.

Chapter

8

"I'd know if I had an infection, wouldn't I?"

The stuff you forgot
from sex-ed class

A Real-Life Dilemma

Sweaty and red-faced, Amanda burst through the door of the girls' locker room. Without a glance in the mirrors, she tightened her silky ponytail while scanning the empty rows: wood benches, scattered books, lost gym socks, but no Erin. Twenty minutes into lacrosse practice, Amanda had been sent on a search and rescue to find the missing team captain. It wasn't like Erin. For the second day in a row, Lakeside High's star player and team leader was a no-show.

Her steady jog staggered to a halt as she reached the last row of lockers. "Mission accomplished," Amanda panted, as she bent forward, pressing her hands to her thighs. "What are you doing in here? Coach says either you'd better be dying of something, or your butt better be on the field in two minutes."

Erin, who was sitting against the wall with her arms wrapped tight around her knees, looked up at Amanda and promptly burst into tears. "I wish I was," she squeaked out between sobs.

"Wish you were what?"

"Dying," she gulped, wiping a hand across her runny nose.

"What in the world are you talking about?" asked Amanda, who took a no-nonsense approach to everything, including life-and-death declarations. She looked over the cocooned body of the usually sturdy, 5-foot 7-inch center. Except for being obviously bummed about something, she looked okay. "Erin, talk to me. What's up?" Amanda flipped open two, three lockers until she located a pack of Kleenex. She plopped down on the floor, opposite the girl, and handed her the tissues.

"I . . . I can't talk about it," she said, burying her head in her knees.

"Did you and Justin have a fight?" As relationships went at Lakeside High, Justin and Erin were a steady romance. She hadn't heard any rumblings of trouble.

"No, but I wish we had, then none of this would have had happened."

"What happened . . . Oh, no, you're not—"

Erin's head popped up, shaking adamantly. "No, I'm not pregnant. I couldn't possibly be. Justin and I, well, we haven't even gone that far. That's what makes this even more unreal."

"Makes what unreal?"

Biting her lip, Erin peeked around Amanda's slim frame. "There's nobody else in here, right?"

"Uh, no. It was just me when I came in looking for you. Seriously, what could be more horrible than getting pregnant?" she grinned, thinking Erin had probably caught Justin flirting with Kristen Shaw.

"Can . . . can you keep a secret, if I tell you something, something really awful?"

"Of course," she said, her expression turning more solemn. It wouldn't be the first time a classmate had confided a problem. Being labeled the class brain, Amanda often found herself in the role of listener, mediator, and general information specialist. "I would never repeat anything you told me. Promise."

Erin nodded, wiping the tears from her face. "I, um, I missed practice the other day because I was at the doctor's, the gynecologist's.

"Uh huh. And?"

"I . . . I thought I had a yeast infection. Some kind of cream-curing, pill-popping, maybe even a shot-in-the-butt kind of infection," she said, looking anywhere except into Amanda's face.

"And that's not what you have?"

"She told me," her eyes finally meeting Amanda's, "that I have herpes. You know, the kind you get down there," she said, her teary eyes darting to Amanda's red and black Lakeside shorts. "Genital herpes," she gulped. "It's insane! I'm a virgin, I swear. How could this happen? I don't sleep around . . . I didn't even sleep with Justin. He's the first real boyfriend I've ever had."

Amanda's brow furrowed tighter with each fact that Erin spewed off. "How is that even possible? If you guys weren't having sex . . . ?"

"We . . . had oral sex," she said in a hushed whisper.

"Oh, I see." Although she didn't have firsthand experience, Amanda had heard enough kids talk about oral sex. It was pretty common. Nobody seemed to think it was such a big deal. "You mean, you caught it from going down on him?"

Erin's head shook again. "That's what I figured, but it was the other way around."

"You mean, when he, um, went down on you . . ." she mumbled, her hand nervously flitting through the air. The topic wasn't really in

Amanda's comfort zone. She preferred to give fashion advice or solve last night's calculus problem, perhaps lend a sympathetic ear to the details of a nasty breakup. This was way different. "Well, no, actually I don't get it. How is that possible?"

"A cold sore."

"A cold sore?" she repeated. "On his mouth? You mean, a regular old cold sore like my grandmother gets?"

"Yep. I know; it's unbelievable! The doctor and I went through the list of ways I might have gotten it. Nothing made sense until she asked if my boyfriend had recently had a cold sore. All it takes is a sore, moisture, and any kind of skin-to-skin contact. And the sore doesn't even have to be visible."

"No way! Oh my God, that's awful!" But then, what Amanda did know about STDs dawned on her. "Erin, I'm so sorry. Genital herpes, that's like forever. It doesn't go away, does it?"

"No, I'll have the virus, like, till I die. The outbreaks, which I can tell you are pretty painful—blisters and stuff—are random," she said, her forehead pounding into her knees again.

Amanda could hardly believe what she was hearing. She'd only known Erin since freshman year. But she was a nice girl: funny, easy-going, a great athlete. It was the kind of story she might have expected to hear about Kristen Shaw or Todd Winters, both known to get around. Things like this didn't happen to girls like her.

"Did, um, did you tell Justin?"

"I don't know what to say to him. We specifically haven't had sex because we didn't want the hassle of birth control or worrying about getting a disease. We thought the oral sex thing was totally cool and safe."

"I . . . I just don't know what to say. But I'm here if you want to talk," Amanda offered.

Erin mustered a grim smile, pulling the last tissue from the package. "Thanks. Listen, there's no way I can make practice. It still hurts pretty bad. Would you tell Coach I was really sick in here or something?"

"Sure, no problem. What . . . what are you going to do now?"

"Well, I don't think I can spend the rest of my life on the floor of the girls' locker room. Head home . . . maybe just drive around, I don't know." She stood, but before walking away, Erin added, "I know it's really awful, but at least I managed to hang on to my virginity. I suppose that's something."

Amanda watched as Erin gathered her lacrosse stick and backpack, offering a sympathetic smile as she disappeared out the door. She let out a deep breath, unable to imagine anything Erin was facing. So many questions: What would she tell Justin? Would she tell her parents? And what about her next boyfriend? She'd have to tell him, wouldn't she? Getting up from the cold tile floor, one more thought occurred to Amanda. Was Erin really still a virgin? Maybe . . . in a technical sort of way, but was it that black and white? She wasn't sure, but it just didn't seem right.

Doc Talk: The Way We See It

SEXUALLY TRANSMITTED DISEASES only happen to other people, right? That's the thinking among most teens. And why not? You're clean, you're smart, you're healthy. That should keep you safe, right? Not at all. Your age-group has more STDs than any other group of people. And in the United States, your age-group has up to SEVENTY (yes, seventy!) times more STDs than teens in European countries. Wow.

So here we go again, telling you to avoid sexual contact altogether or to be smart and protect yourself. Avoiding risky sexual contact and using condoms correctly and consistently with all sexual contact will help protect you physically and emotionally. Physically, avoiding infections or getting them treated early is important for many obvious reasons. STDs can cause pain, infertility, even death. Avoiding them altogether is best, but if you are having sex, the only way to know you are avoiding them is to get tested. And if you learn that you haven't avoided them, then early diagnosis and treatment can reduce and sometimes eliminate the scary complications and consequences.

What about the emotional side of STDs? As doctors who have to deliver the bad news way too often, we see the emotional pain that STDs cause for teen girls. Most girls cry when they are diagnosed with an STD. They say they feel humiliated and dirty. Or they realize that their BF has been unfaithful. They fear infertility or recurrent infections that will affect them for the rest of their lives. And just like Erin, they never ever thought it would happen to them.

When people have sex, STDs happen—especially during the teen years, and especially to those who least expect it. Being prepared and protected is key. Since most of the STDs out there have very mild symptoms (if any at all), there's no way to know for sure who's got what. It means that having sex involves risk. When you become involved in a committed, adult relationship, sometimes that risk seems acceptable to you. You may know that he's had sex with others before you, and you may be willing to accept whatever he brings to your relationship because you're confident he'll be sticking around and committed to you for a long time. But when you're young, the commitment and trust and long-term stuff just aren't there, so the stakes are a lot higher.

This chapter will take you through lots of diseases. Some are worse than others, but none of them are any fun. If you're having sex or getting physical with your guy, there's a lot to learn about staying healthy and disease-free. If you have more questions than we answer here, send them to us through our website (www.girlology.com) and look for the answers there. And once again, we have to say "keep it real." Having sex means you have to be responsible. Take charge of your health and your future. Don't be fooled into thinking that it can't happen to you. **If you're having sex, get serious about protecting yourself, taking care of your body, and getting tested regularly.**

"How many people get STDs per year?"

The Full Scoop: In the United States alone, there are about 19 million new cases of STDs every year. Want a number you can relate to? How about one in four? That's how many teens who have had sex get an STD each year in our country. Sad.

What is the most common STD among teens?

Quickie Answer: HPV and chlamydia.

The Full Scoop: There are two STDs that are extremely common among teens: chlamydia and HPV (human papillomavirus). HPV is the most common. Most of the time, HPV has no symptoms at all, but it can cause genital warts on the vulva, in the vagina, around the anus, or in the throat. It is also the cause of almost all cervical cancer. The creepiest thing about HPV is that if you have symptoms (like warts or an abnormal Pap smear), the virus could have been there for up to a couple years before it even caused any problems. That means if you have sex with more than one person, you may never know for sure exactly when you got it or who you got it from. And because it's a virus, it is treatable but not curable. That means there are treatments (acid, burning, freezing, chemotherapy) that can get rid of the warts and abnormal (precancerous) cells, but the virus stays in your body. But there is good news about HPV. The HPV vaccine can prevent infections and therefore prevent warts, abnormal cells, and cervical cancer. The HPV vaccine is discussed more on page 234.

Chlamydia is the second most common STD among teens. It is curable with antibiotics once the diagnosis is made, but the most challenging thing about chlamydia is that there are usually no symptoms. Most girls have no idea they have it unless they are tested for it at a clinic or doctor's office. **The bad news about chlamydia is that it is the number ONE cause of infertility among women in the United States.** How can an STD make you infertile? Chlamydia doesn't just infect your vagina; it actually infects your cervix and can then move up inside your uterus and fallopian tubes. That's where the damage is done. The pus and infection in there causes scars inside the tubes and uterus. It doesn't mean that one case of chlamydia will definitely make you infertile, but it happens in some cases. And with each new infection, the chances of infertility are higher and higher. For that reason, most doctors are pretty aggressive about testing for chlamydia in teen girls.

Doesn't that suck? The most common STDs usually have no symptoms. How's a girl to know? **No sex? No STD worries. Have sex? Get tested!**

If you ever have chlamydia or any other STDs, there are some things you should do to protect your health and your future fertility:

* Take all of your medication exactly as directed by your doctor. Sometimes a single dose of an antibiotic may be sufficient, and sometimes you have to take it for ten to fourteen days. Whatever is prescribed, take it all—and don't skip any pills!!!

* Tell your partner about your infection so he can get treated. If

you have it, he has it, and he needs treatment. He can go to his doctor or the local health department for treatment.

✳ If (and IF is a big question to consider) you decide to have sex with him again, you MUST use a condom (if you got chlamydia, you probably didn't use a condom every time you had sex . . . right?) and you MUST see written evidence that he was treated or you need to watch him take his medication. Even after you both finish all the medication prescribed, you should make sure you use condoms every time you have sex, and wait at least a week after finishing the medicine before having sex again because it can take that long for the infection to completely clear up. Better yet, take a longer sex holiday!!

✳ Get retested about three months after your treatment to make sure you didn't get infected again.

✳ Get tested if you ever have another sexual partner.

✳ If you remain sexually active, get tested at least every year, and some doctors even recommend every six months, especially if you have more than one sexual partner.

"Will I know if I have an STD?"

Quickie Answer: Probably not.

The Full Scoop: Most people are not aware they have an STD. Why? **Because most of the time, there are NO symptoms in guys or girls who are infected.** If there are symptoms, they can mimic a lot of other things. It's important to remember that the most common and/or the most dangerous STDs frequently have no symptoms. That's chlamydia, HPV, and HIV! So don't think you are infection-free just because you don't have any symptoms that bother you.

Many STDs can take weeks, months, or years before symptoms show. Some people never develop symptoms for some STDs. STDs can still be given to someone else even when a person is not experiencing symptoms.

There are some infections that do have symptoms almost all the time, but the symptoms can be mild and easily ignored or allowed to worsen. Things like molluscum contagiosum, genital herpes, and trichomonas usually cause bumps, painful ulcers, or vaginal itching. **But all those symptoms can be confused with common problems** like bug bites, a yeast infection, or a small cut or scratch on the vulva.

As girls, we can't even SEE most of our vulva without a mirror, and we definitely can't see inside our vagina to our cervix. And even if we could, it might not look abnormal. That means it's really, really, really hard to recognize a sexually transmitted infection. And that means it's really, really, really important to get checked regularly for STDs if you are having sex.

Since STDs can cause infertility, cancer, and even death, it's important to be informed and get treated if you have one. Having sex is a big responsibility, so be responsible if you choose to have sex, including oral or anal sex. Use condoms to reduce your risks, but remember that condoms are not 100 percent effective. That means if you are going to do it, get tested. **Don't pretend you're sure. If you're having sex, you can't pretend about such important things.** We'll say it again. Have sex? Get tested! No sex? No worries.

"How often should I get checked for STDs?"

The Full Scoop: It depends on a couple of different factors. If you are having sex with only one partner and you are absolutely confident that your partner is only having sex with you (and believe us, among teenagers and even among adults sometimes, that is hard to know for sure, no matter how much you trust or love your partner), then you should BOTH be checked for STDs about three months after you start having sex and then again every year. **Even if you are using a condom every single time you have sex, you still need to be tested.** Condoms are the absolutely best way to prevent STDs among people who are having sex, but they are not 100 percent effective in preventing all STDs.

If you EVER have sex without a condom or if you EVER have more than one partner, you are taking big risks, and you need to face that reality. That means you need more frequent testing.

The surest way to prevent STDs is to not have sex. Even though that's what most doctors (including us) recommend for teens, we recognize that a lot of teens don't follow that advice. If you've decided to have sex, you're taking on something that carries a lot of adult responsibility, so you need to act responsibly. That means you take care of yourself and your partner by using a condom correctly every single time you have sex and by only having sex with one person, hopefully someone you love, trust, and share a committed relationship with.

"How does my doctor test for STDs?"

The Full Scoop: There are a few different ways to check for STDs. And it's important to remember that just because you have a pelvic exam doesn't necessarily mean you've been tested. If you want to be tested, make sure you tell your doctor or nurse. The infections that are easily tested for include gonorrhea, chlamydia, trichomonas, syphilis, hepatitis, human papillomavirus, and HIV. Testing for herpes is typically done only if you have a sore on your skin, vulva, or vaginal area because the test involves rubbing a swab on the ulcer.

To test for gonorrhea and chlamydia, your doctor will either use a urine specimen or take a little bit of mucus from your cervix during a pelvic exam by using something like a cotton swab. The swab is sent to a laboratory for the test to be done, and the results usually take a day or two. Again, **don't ASSUME that you are tested just because you give some urine or your doctor does a speculum exam of your vagina.**

To test for trichomonas, your doctor or nurse will need to take a sample of your vaginal discharge and look at it under a microscope or run a special test on it. If your doctor looks under the microscope, you will usually know whether you have trichomonas before you leave the office. Some doctors and nurses, however, send a test off to a lab for the results and that can take longer, but the results should be available within a day.

To test for HIV, syphilis, and hepatitis, you will need to have a tube of blood taken from your arm and sent to a lab. The results take several days to a week in some places. For HIV and hepatitis testing, you need to understand exactly what a "negative" result means. For example, if you test negative for HIV, it really means you were negative up until about six weeks ago, but it doesn't give you any information about whether you might have been infected within the past six weeks. That's because it takes the body at least six weeks to create the antibodies that the test looks for. So if you had unprotected sex in the last six weeks and got HIV, it may not even show up in your blood for six to twelve weeks.

If you are tested shortly after you have sex for the first time, your doctor probably won't test for all STDs, but will test you for the ones that are most common in your area and age-group: gonorrhea, chlamydia, and possibly hepatitis, HIV, and syphilis. There are some other less-common STDs out there that your doctor will specifically test for only if you have symptoms or risk factors for it, like lymphogranuloma venereum and chancroid. To learn more about all the possible STDs, check out the table on page 242 or visit the American Social Health Association website at www.ashastd.org for accurate information.

Wherever you get tested, a nurse or clinic staff member should make sure you know how you will receive the results. They can arrange for you to return to the office to get the results in person or some will agree to call your cell phone or have you call the office. Believe it or not, some parents have called trying to "impersonate" their teens and get results or other confidential health information from doctors. For that reason, some offices and clinics ask you to have a "code word" that confirms that you and only you can get the results. If you worry about your parent trying to get results you want kept private, you can request that they ask for your code word to verify your identity. **Even as a minor, you have the right to confidential care, and your health information cannot be shared even with your parent unless the clinic or doctor has YOUR permission.** Nice, huh? But that also means that you have to be taking responsibility for your own health.

"Which STDs can be cured by treatment?"

Quickie Answer: Bacterial infections are curable; viral infections are not.

The Full Scoop: As you have probably learned over the years, a virus is not curable, but medications can ease the symptoms. A common cold is a good example of a virus. There are no medicines that will make a common cold disappear, but there are different medications to reduce your congestion, ease your cough, help your sore throat, and slow down your runny nose. But if you have a bacterial infection like strep throat (it's caused by a specific bacteria called streptococcus), it is curable with an antibiotic pill or shot. Bacterial infections are usually curable using specific antibiotics, even though it may take a few days for the symptoms to completely disappear.

Myth Bust! You don't have to take all of your medicine!

Think it's okay to stop taking your antibiotics once you feel better? **No way!** Some bacteria die quickly with exposure to an antibiotic for a short time, but others require as much as two weeks or more of antibiotics before the infection is gone. It is ALWAYS important to take all of the antibiotics that come with your prescription, even if you feel fine.

With STDs, it's the same. The most common bacterial STDs include gonorrhea, chlamydia, syphilis, and trichomonas. All of these are easily treated with antibiotics once the diagnosis is made.

If you think you might have trouble taking the medication several times a day or for a long time, you can ask your doctor if a shot would work as well. Painful but effective!

"Are there STDs that are not curable?"

Quickie Answer: Yep.

The Full Scoop: As we said above, the viral infections are not curable, but we can treat the symptoms to ease discomfort or slow the progress of the infection and its complications. And even better, there are vaccines that can *prevent* infection with HPV and hepatitis (see the next question).

The most common viral infections include HPV (human papillomavirus), herpes (HSV or herpes simplex virus), HIV (human immunodeficiency virus), and HBV (hepatitis B virus).

HPV can cause genital warts and cervical cancer. Herpes causes painful blisters and sores that come back over and over for a lifetime. Medications can reduce how often the blisters happen, but there is no treatment that cures the virus, so it just stays in your body. HIV, as you probably know, affects your immune system and causes worsening problems with your ability to fight infection. Eventually, everyone with HIV develops AIDS and dies. Again, there's no cure, but there are medications that can slow down the progress of the disease and allow people living with HIV/AIDS to have a longer and more comfortable life. Finally, hepatitis B infects the liver and affects people in several different ways. Sometimes it just causes a few weeks of illness, while other times it may lead to liver cancer or liver failure, which means a liver transplant is necessary for survival.

Since none of these are curable and they are all very serious, **prevention is key!** The best prevention for all of these infections is to avoid sexual contact (including oral sex). For people having sexual contact, condoms are the best bet for preventing these infections. They have to be used the right way, every time, and during all sexual contact. Sounds tough, but having one of these STDs is much worse.

Vaccines are also important for preventing infection in the first place. They are available for HPV and hepatitis B. If you are vaccinated against these, you won't get infected even if you are exposed to the virus through blood or sexual contact. Learn more about the HPV vaccine in the next question.

"Should I get the HPV vaccine even if I've already had sex?"

Quickie Answer: Yes. But it won't protect you against any of the strains you might have already been infected with.

The Full Scoop: The first available HPV vaccine is a series of three shots that will prevent 70 percent of cervical cancers and 90 percent of genital warts in women. Since about half of all females will be infected with HPV at some point in their lives, and there's no way to know which half you'll be in, the vaccine is recommended for all females.

Even if you have sex with only one person in your life, you could still get HPV if your one guy has had sex with anyone else before you.

The HPV vaccine is recommended for girls who are eleven to twelve years old, and also for all females between twelve and twenty-six years old who have not previously been vaccinated. It protects against four of the most common strains of HPV. There are actually over forty strains of this virus that can infect you, but the four that are targeted by the vaccine are the most common and among the most troublesome.

Since HPV is sexually transmitted, the vaccine works best if you receive it (and that means all three shots in the series) before having any sexual contact. If you've already had sex, there's a chance you may have already been infected with one of the strains of HPV, but the vaccination is still recommended because it can prevent problems related to the strains you don't have. If you have already been infected with one or more of the strains, the vaccine cannot prevent warts or cancers that might arise from that infection. Similarly, if you already have genital warts or an abnormal Pap smear, the vaccine will not treat either of those problems.

Even if you get the HPV vaccine, **you should still have a yearly Pap smear** (starting within three years of becoming sexually active). About 30 percent of cervical cancers are not preventable by the vaccine, so Pap smear screening is the only way to find it early. Early diagnosis is important because it is very curable in the earliest stages.

"What is BV?"

Quickie Answer: BV stands for bacterial vaginosis. It is a vaginal condition that is more common in girls who have sex, but it is not considered a sexually transmitted disease. It will, however, increase your risk for getting other infections, so it should be treated. Read more about it in Chapter 2.

"Can you really get an STD from a toilet seat?"

Quickie Answer: It's not very likely, but anything's possible.

The Full Scoop: Most bacteria and viruses cannot live away from moisture, warmth, and nourishment (fluids from your body). There are some pretty hardy ones, though, that can live for a few hours and even up to a day on inanimate surfaces. Molluscum contagiosum can live on objects for about a day. Pubic lice can live in sheets, clothing, and furniture for about a day. Other than that, you would pretty much have to sit right down on a blob of infected vaginal discharge, a puddle of infected urine, or infected juice from a sore to catch an STD from a toilet seat. **Toilet seats can be pretty yucky, but there aren't many infections you can get from one.** If you face a nasty seat, make sure you squat, don't sit. And don't forget to wash your hands!

"If I have a cold sore, does that mean I have herpes?"

The Full Scoop: Probably. Believe it or not, about 75 percent of American adults have oral herpes. That's right, three out of four. Having oral herpes doesn't mean you got it sexually, though. Most people get oral herpes as children when they are kissed by a relative or friend who has it. Oral herpes can cause "cold sores" inside the mouth and "fever blisters" on the lips. But all of the sores that occur inside the mouth are not necessarily herpes.

If you have a cold sore or fever blister, it is important that you avoid kissing and definitely avoid performing oral sex. **And if your BF has it, don't let him kiss you . . . anywhere!** Oral herpes can infect the genital area of males or females, and it's usually a pretty severe infection when it first occurs. So, if you have a cold sore, make sure you wait until the symptoms are gone and the skin has become completely normal again before you do any kissing or other contact with your mouth.

"How can I keep from getting an infection through oral sex (besides not having oral sex)?"

Quickie Answer: If you're going to have oral sex, the best protection is with a barrier such as a condom or household plastic wrap.

"I have little bumps on my labia and vaginal opening. I'm scared I have an infection."

Quickie Answer: Whatever you have, you need to get it checked out by a doctor.

The Full Scoop: Depending on how closely you are looking at your labia, the bumps may be normal, a sign of an infection, or another abnormality. Rather than describe all the possibilities and let you try to diagnose yourself, **you'll be much better off having your doctor examine the bumps to make an accurate diagnosis.** The possibilities include normal structures on the labia or abnormal things like genital warts, molluscum contagiosum, syphilis, herpes, and precancerous bumps. What? Those are some scary-sounding possibilities. That's why it's important to get an accurate diagnosis. For some information on all these infections, see the table that begins on page 242.

"Is genital herpes really for life?"

Quickie Answer: Unfortunately, it is.

The Full Scoop: Genital herpes is one of those infections that can't be cured. Once you are infected, the virus lives in nerve endings in the area where you had your original outbreak. It tends to recur during times of stress, illness, and sometimes just randomly. The timing is pretty unpredictable, but each recurrent outbreak tends to occur in the same area and show up as a cluster of small, painful ulcers or blisters.

If you have genital herpes, you can usually tell when you're about to have another outbreak because you'll have tingling, burning, or aching in the outbreak area. That's called a prodrome. Some people get outbreaks as frequently as every month and some only get a couple per year.

Whenever there's a prodrome or an outbreak, it's important to avoid all sexual contact because it is easily spread through skin-to-skin contact. The scariest and most frustrating thing about herpes is that **it can also be present and spreading when there are no symptoms of an outbreak at all**—that's called asymptomatic shedding.

Although herpes is not curable, there are medications that can reduce the pain and speed the healing of the blisters. There are also medications that you can take every day (sometimes twice a day is necessary) to decrease the frequency of outbreaks. This is usually recommended if you have outbreaks every couple of months or about six per year.

"What exactly are crabs?"

Quickie Answer: **Pubic lice.**

The Full Scoop: Some girls refer to all STDs as "crabs." But true crabs are little parasites that feed on human blood (they don't live on other animals, just humans). Nice! Do you remember "head lice outbreaks" at your school when you were little? Remember how kids could get infected just by using someone else's hairbrush or borrowing a hat? Well, head lice prefer head hair, and pubic lice prefer . . . you got it . . . pubic hair or other very coarse hair like armpit hair, eyelashes, or beards. Pubic lice don't typically live on heads.

Crabs are usually passed along from one person to another during close physical contact, so bodily fluids aren't an issue here, and condoms don't offer protection. Crabs can live away from a human for about a day, so you can also get crabs off of any surface, like bed linens, furniture, or clothing. If your pubic hair is available, they'll jump on! The major symptom of crabs is itching, and it typically starts about five days after you get them.

"How many teenagers get HIV?"

Quickie Answer: **Way too many.**

The Full Scoop: In the United States, half of all new HIV infections occur in people under age twenty-five; one-fourth occur in people under the age of twenty-one. Because most teens don't even get tested for HIV, the actual number of teens living with HIV is unknown, but probably higher than you think.

"Isn't syphilis extinct?"

Quickie Answer: **No. Especially not in the South.**

The Full Scoop: Syphilis is a sexually transmitted bacterial infection that is very treatable, but like many other STDs, has symptoms that are often overlooked or ignored. If left untreated, syphilis will progress through three stages that become increasingly more serious. Today, it is almost always diagnosed before the late stage, when it can cause permanent blindness, insanity, and paralysis.

Syphilis is diagnosed by a simple blood test. Like with HIV, if you are infected with syphilis, it may take up to a few months before your blood test will detect it. So a negative test may be wrong if an infection occurred recently. It is one of the conditions that all pregnant women are tested for because it can have devastating effects on a fetus if the mother has the infection during her pregnancy. In many areas of the country, syphilis is very rare, but over half of all the cases in the United States occur in the Southeast.

"What STDs should I worry about if I have sex?"

Quickie Answer: All of them.

The Full Scoop: The table on the next page provides a list of the STDs that you should be aware of if you choose to have sex. **Remember that the best way to prevent ALL of these is to not have sex.** If you choose to have sex, the best prevention is to have sex with only one partner who is not infected and to use a latex condom from the moment there is skin-to-skin contact until there is no skin-to-skin contact. If you are having oral sex (giving or receiving), you still need to protect yourself by using a barrier like an unlubricated condom or even plastic wrap.

STD	How you get it	Symptoms	Diagnosis	Curable	Complications
Chancroid	Skin-to-skin contact with an open sore	In females, there is a painless ulcer or sore. There may be enlarged lymph nodes.	Testing (culture) of fluid or cells from the ulcer or sore	Yes, with antibiotics	May cause severely infected glands that need surgery to remove. Increased risk of HIV transmission.
Chlamydia	Vaginal, oral, or anal contact. The penis does not have to go inside the vagina.	Usually none. May cause vaginal spotting or a change in vaginal discharge	Testing a specimen from infected area (cervix, mouth, anus) or urine	Yes, with antibiotics	PID Menstrual pain Chronic pelvic pain Infertility Increased risk of HIV transmission. Untreated infants (infected during birth) can develop blindness.
Crabs (Pubic lice)	Contact with pubic hair, bedsheets, towels, or other surfaces that crabs may be living on	Itching	Finding lice or lice eggs in the pubic hair. These lice do not usually live on head hair.	Yes, with prescription or over-the-counter solutions	

STD (con't)	How you get it	Symptoms	Diagnosis	Curable	Complications
Gonorrhea	Vaginal, oral, or anal contact. The penis does not have to go inside the vagina.	May have none. May have vaginal spotting or a change in vaginal discharge	Testing a specimen from infected area (cervix, mouth, anus) or urine	Yes, with antibiotics	PID Menstrual pain Chronic pelvic pain Infertility Miscarriage Blindness in infants born to an infected mother Severe infection throughout the body including the joints, heart, brain, and blood
Hepatitis B	Contact with infected blood, semen, or vaginal fluids	May have none. Vague flulike symptoms (tired, stomach pain, nausea, vomiting, loss of appetite) May develop jaundice (yellow skin and eyes) May have a rash	Blood test	No PREVENTABLE by vaccination	Incurable infection Damaged liver Liver cancer Death

STD (con't)	How you get it	Symptoms	Diagnosis	Curable	Complications
Herpes	Skin-to-skin contact, particularly with the mouth or genital areas	May have none Most commonly shows up as a cluster of small, painful blisters Painful urination First outbreaks may also have fever, enlarged lymph nodes, flulike symptoms.	Culture from the sore or lesion Blood tests are available if there are no symptoms or the lesions have already healed. Some blood tests are not accurate.	No There are medications to reduce the symptoms.	Recurrent sores that happen randomly over a lifetime Chronic pain Increased risk of HIV transmission (giving and getting) Neonatal herpes is rare but serious. It occurs in babies who are infected during pregnancy or birth.
HIV/AIDS	Contact with infected bodily fluids including semen, vaginal fluid, anal fluids, blood, and breast milk. Contact can be sexual, blood transfusion, organ transplant, injection drug use with shared needles	None until the disease begins to progress toward AIDS. This may take years after the initial infection, but the person is still able to infect others.	The presence of HIV is determined by a blood test. The diagnosis of AIDS is made by a physician and based on the presence of certain illnesses.	No Medications can prolong life and improve the quality of life by controlling symptoms temporarily.	Inability to fight off infections, even mild ones that a healthy body can prevent Infections that are resistant to treatment Cancers Death

STD (con't)	How you get it	Symptoms	Diagnosis	Curable	Complications
HPV	Skin-to-skin contact	Usually no symptoms. Symptoms may take 6 weeks to several years to show up. May have warts or bumps on the vulva, vagina, cervix May show up as an abnormal Pap smear	Usually by typical appearance or by biopsy Special DNA tests can be used to determine if HPV is present on the cervix.	No PREVENTABLE by vaccination Warts and abnormal cells can be removed using chemicals, freezing, burning, or surgery.	Warts Cervical cancer Cancer of the vulva Vocal chord polyps May come back after treatment
Molluscum	Contact with skin or objects where the virus is present	Raised, flesh-colored bumps that usually have a tiny dimple in the center. They may be painless, or they may itch.	Based on the way they look Can be made by a biopsy	Yes, with removal Will eventually go away on their own in healthy individuals	Scars In people infected with HIV, it can spread all over the body and be untreatable.

STD	How you get it	Symptoms	Diagnosis	Curable	Complications
PID (pelvic inflammatory disease)	Bacteria, usually chlamydia or gonorrhea, in the cervix or vagina, move into the uterus, fallopian tubes, and ovaries.	Pelvic pain Fever Nausea/vomiting Bleeding between periods Painful sex May have increased or abnormal discharge May have no symptoms	Based on findings during a physical exam May be based on how the reproductive structures look at the time of a surgery (scars and scar tissue)	Yes with antibiotics May require surgery if the infection is not getting better with antibiotics	Infertility Increased chances of tubal pregnancy Chronic pelvic pain from scar tissue Untreated PID can result in severe infections that spread throughout the body and can be life-threatening.
Trichomonas	Contact with infected semen or vaginal fluids	There may be no symptoms. Vaginal itching Discharge that is green, gray, or yellow and may have a bad odor Burning with urination Burning during or after sex	A sample of vaginal discharge is placed in a drop of saline and viewed under the microscope. The pH of the vagina may be checked to help with the diagnosis.	Yes, with antibiotics	Increases the risk of transmitting HIV (giving and getting) May contribute to pregnancy complications like preterm birth

STD (con't)	How you get it	Symptoms	Diagnosis	Curable	Complications
Syphilis	Skin-to-skin contact with an infected sore, usually during vaginal, oral, or anal sex. The penis does not have to go inside the vagina.	Symptoms differ based on the stage of the infection, but all of the symptoms will go away on their own without treatment while the infection continues to stay in the body and cause harm. First symptom: a painless, raised sore called a chancre on the genital area, lips, or in the mouth Secondary stage: rash on the hands and feet, raised, wartlike growths in the genital area or round white lesions in the mouth	Blood test Looking at fluid from a chancre under a special microscope Testing the fluid taken from around the spinal cord	Yes, with antibiotics if treated before the final stages	Untreated syphilis can lead to blindness, problems with the heart, brain, blood vessels; and finally to insanity and paralysis.

Think It Through

Think It Through

Think It Through

Chapter

"What Happened to Chelsea and Zach?"

An update

A Real-Life Dilemma

Chelsea came bounding from the sidelines of a late October football game and straight into Zach's arms. She was exhausted, hoarse from cheering, and her thighs had gone numb by the end of the third quarter. The moment she kissed him, it all melted away. He could do that. One kiss, one touch made her forget everything around her.

She loved that he wasn't on the football team. Zach was more of a track-and-field, Frisbee-throwing guy with lanky muscles—not particularly interested in heavy contact sports. Chelsea knew he'd only shown up to watch her cheer. He was attentive in all the right places, and she had to admit, initially, it was part of what had attracted her to him. But as the months passed, it was way more than that. Zach was smart and funny and oh-so-cute. Maybe not in an obvious Aidan Scofield way, but subtly, with intense brown eyes and dark waves of hair she thought she could get lost in. And best of all, he felt the same way about her, a connection that surpassed ordinary Lakeside High romances.

Zach spun them both around, kissing her again, her feet dangling a foot off the ground. He was much taller, his 6-foot body towering over Chelsea's petite 5-foot, 1-inch frame. Well, nothing was perfect. "Are you done cheering the Panthers on to victory?" he asked, tucking her head beneath his chin.

"Done for this week. Do you want to run away to Hawaii or Mexico?" It was a game they played on a daily basis, ditching Lakeside High, parents, and their friends for a life on the run. They knew they'd never do it, but sometimes it was fun to play with the future. "I vote Mexico. I'm starving," she said. "When we get there can I get a burrito?"

"You," he said, holding her tight, "can have anything you want."

"What if I want you?"

"You already have me."

Chelsea grabbed his arm, halting Zach's long strides. "All of you. What if I want to have sex with you?" The game quieted.

"Whoa, I thought we put that conversation away for a while." Giving her a quizzical look, Zach took her hand as they crossed the soggy field. She didn't say anything more as they reached the parking lot. "Chel, you've stopped talking," he said, while opening her door.

As he got in the driver's side, Chelsea realized she was holding her breath. In one big gulp she blurted it out. "I made a decision, that's all. Absolutely," she said, nodding hard, "Let's do it. Let's have sex. I'm sure I'm ready." Zach's mouth dropped open, his head clunking against the window. He seemed a little stunned. Usually, after a game, she talked about how lame the other team's cheerleaders were or how their own captain, Michelle Finch, was out of sync—again.

But it shouldn't have been a total shocker. They'd been talking about it—on and off—for months. Every conversation ended with no . . . yes . . . I'll think about it . . . stop . . . go . . . maybe. And he'd been so sweet, Chelsea had almost said yes for that reason alone. He didn't pressure her, said he'd hang around forever, until they were both ready. A few weeks before he'd suggested they forget about sex for a while. That bothered her. First he was willing to forget about sex, next he'd probably forget about her. Maybe he was losing interest.

"Chelsea, are you sure?" he asked, interrupting her mental debate. "We've waited this long."

"You mean *I've* waited this long." Zach sighed, looking out the window.

Sometimes Chelsea was sorry he'd ever told her. Last year, long before they'd started dating, Zach had done it—had sex with Kayla Jensen. He and Kayla had only been dating a month. Chelsea tried not to let that nasty fact influence her, but it still bugged her. Sitting behind Kayla in English, Chelsea couldn't concentrate, thinking, *You've had sex with my boyfriend—and I haven't*. However, she was smart enough to realize it wasn't a good enough reason for her to have sex with Zach. "Sorry, I shouldn't have brought it up."

It was too late. "How many ways can I say it? It was a mistake. I never felt this way about her—you know that, Chelsea. I admit I was a willing participant, but it was her idea. That's one of the things I love about you. A lot of girls, like Kayla, wouldn't give sex this much thought. This is so important to you. And I might be the guy who's important enough to do it with. That's all I need to know."

"But I thought . . ."

"You thought what?"

"Well," she said, looking anywhere but at him. "A couple of weeks ago, you said you didn't want to talk about sex anymore. I just figured you were getting tired of waiting. Plenty of girls would love to sleep with you, Zach. I get that. There has to be more, eventually—I mean, how long are you going to be happy with just kissing me?"

He closed his eyes and reached over, doing just that. "Um, at least another seven to ten days," he said, laughing. Opening his eyes, Zach took in her serious expression. "Okay, maybe we need to talk about this some more."

"What's the problem? I said yes."

"Why? Because it's the perfect next step for us—or because you're afraid of what's going to happen if we don't do it?" Chelsea opened her mouth to reply, but he gently put a finger to her lips. "Just hear me out while I'm thinking straight." With a waffling gulp, Zach's eyes gazed over her. "You know, Chel, I am only human." He cleared his throat. "First, I can tell you that while there's that momentary burst of, um, pleasure with sex, there's a lot of hours you spend thinking about other stuff—later."

"You mean like when Syd and Aidan had sex? Remember, I told you how Sydney felt afterward, just kind of empty. It wouldn't be that way for us; we're not them. We've been dating for seven months. They only did it out of curiosity."

"It's not just that, Chel. Listen, I know you don't like to talk about it. But, well, with Kayla, she was late—her period," he said, his glance darting away.

Chelsea's eyes bugged wide, her body stiffening against the seat as her hand pulled away from his. He didn't say anything else for a moment and her imagination ran wild. "You said you used a condom," she whispered.

"We did," he insisted. "And that feeling you have right now—angry, scared—multiply it by a thousand. That's how I spent about five days last year."

"And?" Chelsea said, now convinced she was going to have to transfer to another English class.

"And it turned out to be nothing, just a scare. The point is, I don't want you to have to go through something like that. Let me tell you, it sucks. I know I love you, but we're not ready for anything like that."

"You must have been so relieved."

"Ah, yeah, relieved doesn't quite cover it. I can promise that you and I would definitely use more effective birth control, but there's always going to be a risk. Is that something you're ready to worry about every time we have sex? And I know you, Chelsea, you're a worrier."

He had her there. Chelsea agonized over most things: what her friends thought of her new jeans, schoolwork, next week's game, whether or not she needed to lose five pounds. Those things were probably nothing compared to the fear of an unwanted pregnancy. "If something like that were to happen, it would be a lot of pressure to do the right thing—especially because it is us. It wouldn't be an easy decision."

"Hey, I'm glad it wouldn't be an easy decision," he said, tipping his forehead against hers. "But if we wait, it's one less complication, one less thing to worry about for now. You know, Chel, I don't have a perfect answer. But I have figured out this much—sex won't make our relationship any stronger. It's waiting that's going to prove what you and I have in the long run."

Chelsea smiled, throwing her arms around him. "I can't believe I'm saying this, but I think you're right."

Doc Talk:
The Way **We See It**

THINK IT THROUGH. MAKE SMART CHOICES. Chelsea and Zach did.

Epilogue

Tasha, Chelsea, Amanda, and Sydney all struggled, at times, to make the right choices, just like you and your friends. It wasn't always easy to do the right thing, and sometimes they didn't. What's important is they considered the options, thought it through, and talked things out with someone they trusted. Maybe they even read this book. We like to think, perhaps, they bookmarked a page or two and highlighted some points for future reference. Maybe someday they'll get into a situation and remember that they once saw the answer to their problem right here.

So what did happen to them? Did Chelsea and Zach decide to chuck suburbia and head for the Mexican border after all? Maybe Sydney ended up on *American Idol,* and Aidan Scofield ended up idolizing her from afar. Wouldn't that be sweet? Perhaps Amanda and Tasha won Ivy League scholarships and went on to medical school. Years later, they decided to team up and write a smart, hip book on hang-ups, hook-ups, and holding out. Well, anything's possible. But realistically, we think their futures went something like this:

Tasha never did go on a date with Ty Johnson, too worried that his ego might be too big for the both of them. They flirted, remained friends, and parted ways after high school. Tasha didn't follow her mother into medicine, but took a career cue from her dad instead. She graduated from college and continued on to law school. Her firm was eventually hired to represent a major sporting goods chain. No one was more surprised than Tasha when the chain's new executive vice president, Ty Johnson, showed up to a meeting. He looked hotter in a suit than he ever did in basketball shorts. His ego had deflated considerably and his personality matured amazingly well. Equally struck was Ty, blown away by a girl he once thought of as too high-maintenance for him. Tasha and Ty are planning a spring wedding.

Sydney found a late love of art and took to sculpting nudes. After college, she moved to Greenwich Village where her work has appeared at several small gallery showings throughout the Tri-State area. She lives in a studio apartment with two cats, a box turtle, and a goldfish. Sydney's dated a number of fascinating men over the years, none piquing her interest quite as much as her independent lifestyle or her art. She's happy to wait for the right guy to come along, and if he doesn't, that's okay too. However, she just did accept a date with a New York City cop. He was kind enough to rescue one of her cats from an air conditioning duct. Kindness is a quality that Sydney holds in particularly high regard. As for Aidan Scofield, he did show up to their high school reunion, which left Syd with a blush and a smile. It seems Aidan Scofield came with his wife, who looked remarkably like Sydney.

After changing her major six times, Amanda finally settled on health sciences and became a nutritionist. She went to work for a cruise ship line, designing healthy menu substitutes for their gourmet meals. Oddly, she didn't find this line of work terribly rewarding, and when they docked near Los Angeles, she jumped ship. A Hollywood film crew happened to be filming there that day. When the director spotted Amanda, he immediately cast her in a small but pivotal role, claiming she was one of the most beautiful women he'd ever seen. Big surprise. But, by then, Amanda had learned to take her looks in stride and decided to capitalize on them. Though it was never a dream to which she aspired, Amanda is currently filming episodes for her hit television series. But she has even bigger plans for her newfound fame. During hiatus, she's going on a motivational speaking tour designed to help teenage girls cope with the social and academic pressures of high school.

Ah, we bet you wish Chelsea and Zach married and lived happily ever after. We wish we could say it was so. But Chelsea and Zach eventually grew apart and went their separate ways—because, most of the time, that's the way it goes. (*Ever after* really comes much later.) But not to worry, it all worked out fine. Chelsea attended a large Southern university where she naturally spent four years cheering for the football team. After college, she fell madly in love with Jeff, who owned a small Mexican restaurant. Well, the business took off and the restaurant expanded into a successful chain. Chelsea helps out part-time, but mostly she's a stay-at-home mom, taking care of their three children. Number four is on the way. But before the baby is born—and she swears it's the last one—Chelsea is planning a reunion trip. It's a girls' getaway to Acapulco with Amanda, Tasha, and Sydney, because a third-grade pinky swear and friends like them really can last forever.

The End

References

Abma, J.C., Martinez, G.M, Mosner, W.D. & Dawson, B.S. (2004). *Teenagers in the United States: Sexual Activity, Contraceptive Use and Childbearing, 2002. Vital Health Statistics.* 23(24).

Bearman, P.S., Bruckner H. Promising the future: Virginity pledges and first intercourse. *Am J Sociol.* 2001; 106;859-912.

Centers for Disease Control and Prevention (CDC). *Trends in reportable sexually transmitted diseases in the United States, 2004: National surveillance data for Chlamydia, Gonorrhea, and Syphillis.* Atlanta: CDC, 2005.

Cervical Cancer screening in adolescents. ACOG Committee Opinion No. 300. American College of Obstetricians and Gynecologists. *Obstet Gynecol* 2004;104:885-9.

Collaborative Group on Hormonal Factors in Breast Cancer. Breast cancer and hormonal contraceptives: Collaborative reanalysis of individual data on 53,297 women with breast cancer and 100,239 women without breast cancer from 54 epidemiological studies. *Lancet.* 1996; 347:1713–1727.

Dailard, C., Richardson, C.T. *Teenagers' Access to Confidential Reproductive Health Services, The Guttmacher Report on Public Policy.* November 2005:8(4).

Eugene A, Eugene L. *Contemporary Diagnosis and Management of Attention Deficit/ Hyperactive Disorder.* Newton, PA: Handbooks and Healthcare; 2002.

Girl and Drugs. *A New Analysis: Recent Trends, Risk Factors, and Consequences.* Office of National Drug Control Policy, Executive Office of the President, February 9, 2006. www.mediacampaign.org.

Grunbaum JA et al. Youth risk behavior surveillance, United States, 2003. *Morbidity & Mortality Weekly Report Surveillance Summaries.* 2004; 53(SS-2):1-95.

Guttmacher Institute. *Sex and America's Teenagers.* New York: Guttmacher Institute; 1994.

Hankinson SE, Colditz GA, Hunter DJ, et al. A quantitative assessment of oral contraceptive use and risk of ovarian cancer. *Obstetrics and Gynecology.* 1992; 80(4):708–714.

Hatcher RA, Trussell J, Stewart FH, Nelson AL, Cates W Jr, Guest F, Kowal D, eds. *Contraceptive Technology.* 18th rev. ed. New York: Ardent Media, Inc.; 2004.

Haveman, R.H., Wolfe, B., & Peterson, E. Children of Early Childbearers as Young Adults. In R.A. Maynard (Ed.), *Kids Having Kids: Economic Cost and Social Consequences of Teen Pregnancy* (pp257-284). Washington, DC: The Urban Press; 1997.

Henshaw, SK. Unintended Pregnancy in the Unites States. *Family Planning Perspectives* 1998; 30(1):24-29, 46.

Kirby D. *Emerging Answers: Research Findings on Programs to Reduce Teen Pregnancy,* Washington, DC: National Campaign to Prevent Teen Pregnanc; 2001.

Marchbanks PA, McDonald JA, Wilson HG, et al. Oral contraceptives and the risk of breast cancer. *New England Journal of Medicine.* 2002; 346(26):2025–2032.

Maynard, R.A., (Ed.). *Kids having Kids: A Robin Hood Foundation Special Report on the Cost of Adolescent Childbearing.* New York: Robin Hood Foundation; 1996.

McNeely C. Shew M., Beuhring T, et al. Mothers' influence on the timing of first sex among 14 and 15 year olds. *Journal of Adolescent Health. 2002;3:* 256.

Menstruation in girls and adolescents: using the menstrual cycle as a vital sign. ACOG Committee Opinion No. 349. American Academy of Pediatrics; American College of Obstetricians and Gynecologists. *Obstet Gynecol.* 2006;108:1323-8.

National Campaign to Prevent Teen Pregnancy. *Not Just For Girls: The Roles of Boys and Men in Teen Pregnancy.* Washington, DC: The National Campaign to Prevent Teen Pregnancy; 1997.

National Campaign to Prevent Teen Pregnancy. *With One Voice: America's Adults and Teens Sound Off About Teen Pregnancy.* Washington, DC: The National Campaign to Prevent Teen Pregnancy; 2003.

Office of National AIDS Policy. *Youth and HIV/AIDS 2000: A New American Agenda.* Washington, DC: White House; 2000.

Santelli JS, Lindberg LD, Finer LB, et al. Explaining Recent Declines in Adolescent Pregnancy in the United States: The Contribution of Abstinence and Improved Contraceptive Use. *American Journal of Public Health.* 2007;97(1):150-156.

Sax, Leonard. *Why Gender Matters: What Parents and Teachers Need to Know About the Emerging Science of Sex Differences.* New York: Doubleday; 2005.

Sexually Transmitted Dieases in Adolescents. ACOG Committee Opinion No. 301. American College of Obstetricians and Gynecologists. *Obstet Gynecol.* 2004;104:891-8.

The initial reproductive health visit. ACOG Committee Opinion No. 335. American College of Obstetricians and Gynecologists. *Obstet Gynecol.* 2006;107:1215-9.

Walsh, David. *Why Do They Act That Way? A Survival Guide to the Adolescent Brain for You and Your Teen.* New York: Free Press; 2004.

Weinstock H, et al. Sexually transmitted diseases among American youth: Incidence and prevalence estimates, 2000. *Perspectives on Sexual and Reproductive Health.* 2004; 36(1):6–10.

Whitehead B, Pearson M. *Making a Love Connection: Teen Relationships, Pregnancy, and Marriage.* Washington, DC: National Campaign to Prevent Teen Pregnancy; 2006.

Workowski KA, et al. *Sexually Transmitted Diseases Treatment Guidelines, 2006. Morbidity & Mortality Weekly Report.* August 4, 2006 Vol.55 No. RR-11

Resources

Advocates for Youth
2000 M St NW, Suite 750
Washington, DC 20036
www.advocatesforyouth.org

Alan Guttmacher Institute
120 Wall Street, 21st Floor
New York, NY 10005
www.guttmacher.org

American Academy of Family Physicians
11400 Tomahawk Creek Parkway
Leawood, KS 66211
www.aafp.org

American Academy of Pediatrics
141 Northwest Point Boulevard
Elk Grove Village, IL 60007
www.aap.org

American College of Obstetricians and
    Gynecologists
409 12th Street, SW
PO Box 96920
Washington, DC 20090
www.acog.org

American Social Health Association
PO Box 13827 Research Triangle Park,
NC 27709
www.ashastd.org

Centers for Disease Control &
    Prevention
1600 Clifton Road,
Atlanta, FA 30333
www.cdc.gov

The National Campaign to Prevent
    Teen Pregnancy.
1776 Massachusetts Ave., NW
Suite 200
Washington, DC 20036
www.teenpregnancy.org

National Center for Victims of Crime
    Dating Violence Resource Center
2000 M Street, NW, Suite 480
Washington, DC 20036
www.ncvc.org

National Institute on Alcohol Abuse and
    Alcoholism
5635 Fishers Lane, MSC 9304
Bethesda, MD 20892-9304
www.niaaa.nih.gov

National Institute on Drug Abuse /
    NIDA for Teens
6001 Executive Boulevard, Room 5213
Bethesda, MD 20892-9561
www.teens.drugabuse.gov

National Institute of Mental Health
6001 Executive Boulevard, Room 8184,
MSC 9663
Bethesda, MD 20892-9663
http://www.nimh.nih.gov

Planned Parenthood Federation of
    America, Inc.
434 W 33rd St.
New York, NY 10001
www.plannedparenthood.org

Sexuality Information and Education
    Council of the United States
130 West 42nd Street, Suite 350
New York, NY 10036
www.siecus.org

Society for Adolescent Medicine
1916 Copper Oaks Circle
Blue Springs, MO 64015
www.adolescenthealth.org

Acknowledgments

It has been well established that *connection* is the most effective protector of our teens as they navigate adolescence. We believe that connectedness has also helped us navigate our journey through *Hang-Ups, Hook-Ups, and Holding Out.*

For our connections at HCI, we are grateful. Our editor, Allison Janse, built the links that allowed us our freedom yet maintained the perfect balance of support, guidance, and limits. Editing sounds a lot like parenting; we hope we've behaved! We are particularly grateful for Kelly Maragni's friendship, enthusiasm, and the instant connectedness we felt with her in New Orleans. We also appreciate the efforts of everyone else at HCI who has helped get this book into your hands, especially Paola Fernandez, Kim Weiss, and of course, Peter Vegso, for believing in Girlology.

Reconnections count, too. This book would not be what it is without the assistance of Laura Spinella, who provided her expertise as a writer, a mother, and an amazing friend. We have been thrilled by her ability to create the characters and the scenes that will build another great connection with our readers.

We also appreciate the girls who worked with us on content and voice: Rachel Neil, Vaugn Connolly, Sallie Johnson, Jenny Carter, Aubrey Freudenberger, Anna Sanders, Liz Jackson, and Susannah Nelson.

And lastly, to our families who are so incredibly patient and supportive: we love you and know that our connections with you are the most important of all. To Gayle Cameron, we love your wisdom. Thanks Michael, Anne Claire, Maehler. Steve, Emily, Caroline, and Ella. And to our parents, Hiram and Linda; Eric and Marian; many, many thanks.

Index

Dr. Holmes and Dr. Hutchison **like to talk,** and they talk a lot: to young girls, teens, college groups, parents' groups, politicians, educators, faith leaders, sales people and pretty much anyone who will listen. **But they listen a lot, too**—especially to the teens they get to spend time with through their seminars and website. As sought-after speakers on topics of teen culture, sex education, and promoting healthy sexuality among today's youth, they travel the country helping girls and the adults who care about them start **conversations that matter** about sex and all the stuff that goes along with it. There's a lot to talk about, so why not get the conversations started? As the cofounders of Girlology® and coauthors of *Girlology: A Girl's Guide to Stuff That Matters* and now *Hang-Ups, Hook-Ups and Holding Out,* this duo has the knowledge, the experience, and the nerve to say it the way it needs to be said.

Dr. Melisa Holmes is a magna cum laude graduate of the University of Georgia and a graduate of the Medical College of Georgia. Following her ob-gyn internship and residency at the Medical College of Virginia, Melisa joined the faculty at the Medical University of South Carolina (MUSC), where she held joint appointments in obstetrics/gynecology and pediatrics, and was named among the best doctors in America. During her twelve years of clinical practice, she was director of the MUSC Teen Clinic and founder and director of a clinic for sexual assault survivors. As a nationally recognized advocate for adolescent health, she has served on the American College of Obstetrics and Gynecology Committee on Adolescent Health Care and the National Campaign to Prevent Teen Pregnancy. She has written numerous scientific papers as well as text book chapters on subjects related to adolescent gynecology and women's health. In the medical community, she is a nationally recognized speaker on topics of adolescent gynecology, teen sexuality, and interpersonal violence. Currently, she devotes full time to writing and lecturing for Girlology, organizing the family calendar, and hanging out with her very handsome husband and three incredible daughters.

Dr. Trish Hutchison graduated cum laude from the College of Charleston and earned her MD at the Medical University of South Carolina (MUSC). After completing her pediatrics internship and residency at Vanderbilt University in Nashville, Tennessee, Trish returned to Charleston, where she was in private practice with Charleston Pediatrics for ten years. As a popular physician with adolescent girls in particular, her commitment and passion for adolescent health care grew. She subsequently founded and directed a young women's health center for the Department of Adolescent Medicine at MUSC. As a trusted expert on adolescent development, teen sexuality, and parenting she, too, has been listed among the best doctors in America. She has an engaging and honest approach with teens and at the same time earns their parents' unwavering respect. Currently, she devotes full time to Girlology lectures and programming, but she has a great sense of balance that keeps her plugged into family time and community service. She particularly enjoys volunteering through her church and organizations serving women and children. She lives in Mt. Pleasant, South Carolina, with her very handsome husband and two young but amazing daughters who will keep her studying girlology for many years to come.

Visit **www.girlology.com**

Code #2955 • paperback • $12.95

Get the ultimate straight-talk book for teen girls.

Written with insight, humor, and straight-from-the-hip advice from one who's been there and done that.

Surviving Your Parents' Divorce

The BRIGHT SIDE

Max Sindell

Code #625X • $12.95

Picture Perfect

What You Need to Feel Better About Your Body

Jill S. Zimmerman Rutledge, M.S.W., LCSW

Code #6071 • $14.95

Picture Perfect is an honest and practical guide to help you cope with the hard issue of body image.